J. J Smith

In Eastern Seas

The commission of H. M. S.

J. J Smith

In Eastern Seas
The commission of H. M. S.

ISBN/EAN: 9783337167950

Printed in Europe, USA, Canada, Australia, Japan

Cover: Foto ©ninafisch / pixelio.de

More available books at **www.hansebooks.com**

IN EASTERN SEAS;

OR,

THE COMMISSION OF

H.M.S. "IRON DUKE,"

Flag-ship in China, 1878–83.

BY

J. J. SMITH, N.S.

DEVONPORT:
PRINTED AND PUBLISHED BY A. H. SWISS, 111 AND 112 FORE STREET.
1883.

To my late Shipmates

IN

H.M.S. "IRON DUKE,"

The following pages are respectfully inscribed.

Those who voyage beyond sea change their climate often, but their affections never.

PREFACE.

To write something which shall please one's own friends is one thing; to undertake the task of pleasing anybody else is another; and, I take it, a far more difficult one. The writer of the following pages never sought to sail beyond the peaceful and well-marked area of the first, until induced—at the suggestions of his shipmates, though against his better judgment—to venture on the dark and tempest-swept ocean of the second.

The only originality claimed for the narrative is that of introducing such a manifestly inferior production to your notice.

Shipmates, my little bark is frail; deal gently with her, and—let me ask it as a special favor—do not blow too fiercely on her untried sails.

Much depends on the title of a book. Does it convey an adequate idea of the subject-matter? I would claim for mine at least that merit; for is not every sea over which we have voyaged to the eastward of England?

CONTENTS.

CHAPTER I.
We Commission our Ship—Visit Portsmouth—Prepare to Sail . . . 1

CHAPTER II.
Good-by to Albion—Southward Ho!—Gibraltar 12

CHAPTER III.
Up the Mediterranean—Malta 26

CHAPTER IV.
Port Said—The Suez Canal—Voyage down the Red Sea—Aden 39

CHAPTER V.
Across the Indian Ocean—Ceylon—Singapore—A Cruise in the Straits of Malacca 47

CHAPTER VI.
Sarawak—Labuan—Manilla—Heavy weather . . . 62

CHAPTER VII.
Hong Kong—Some Chinese manners and customs . . 71

CHAPTER VIII.
Preparations for the North—Amoy—Wosung, and what befell us there 83

CHAPTER IX.
Arrival at Nagasaki—Something about Japan—A run through the Town—Visit to a Sintoo Temple . . 94

CHAPTER X.

The Inland Sea—Kobé—Fusi-Yama—Yokohama—Visit to Tokio 113

CHAPTER XI.

Northward—Hakodadi—Dui—Castries Bay—Barracouta—Vladivostock 131

CHAPTER XII.

Chefoo—Nagasaki *en route*—Japan revisited—Kobé—Yokohama 146

CHAPTER XIII.

We attempt an overland route, with the result of the trial . 159

CHAPTER XIV.

The new regime—Something about Saigon—The First Cruise of the China Squadron—An Alarm of Fire!—Arrival of Flying Squadron 181

CHAPTER XV.

Second Cruise of the China Squadron—Principally concerning a Visit to the Loo-Choo Isles and Corea—Welcome news from home—Conclusion 210

APPENDIX A.—Deaths during the Commission . . i.

APPENDIX B.—Table of places visited and distances run during the Commission . . . . . iii.

CHAPTER I.

"We sail the ocean blue,
And our saucy ship's a beauty."

WE COMMISSION OUR SHIP.   VISIT PORTSMOUTH.
PREPARE TO SAIL.

ON one of those delicious semi-tropical afternoons, which geologists tell us once bathed the whole of our island, and which even now, as though loath to part from its one-time home, still dwells lovingly in Devonia's summer, I wended my way to Devonport Park to feast my eyes once again on the familiar scenes of early days. What I beheld was a fair picture—the Hamoaze, with its burden of shapely hulls, and its beautiful undulating shores of wood and dell, lay glittering resplendent at my feet. So still and peaceful was it all that the din of hammers, the whir of machinery, and the voices of men were all blended in one most musical cadence. Scores of pleasure-boats dot the lake-like surface of the noble sheet of water, for the most part rowed by the lusty arms of those amphibious creatures familiarly known as "Jack Tars," recently let loose from the dear old "Model" or the equally dear "Academy." A voice, bell-like and clear—surely that of a girl—invited my closer attention; and yes, there she is! and not one only, but many ones,—one in each boat, whom Jack is initiating into that wonderfully difficult branch of navigation—a sailor's courtship!

Now, whatever anybody else may say to the contrary, I hold that the British tar would scarcely be the "soaring soul" that he is were it not for the influence—not always a beneficial influence, by the way, of the softer sex. And here, a word for him with special respect to what people are pleased to call his inconstancy. With all his vagaries, and from the very nature of his calling he has many, I think there are few other professions which would bear weighing in the balance with his and not be found as wanting in this quality. True, none is so easily swayed, so easily led; but the fault is not his, *that* must be laid at the doors of those who compel England's sailors to a forced banishment for long periods of years, in lands where it is impossible the home influences can reach them. Is it a matter of much wonderment, then, if he is swayed by the new and intoxicating forms which pleasure takes in those far-distant climes where the eye of Mrs. Grundy never penetrates?

A somewhat curious way in which to commence my narrative, say you? I think so too, on re-reading it; but with your permission, I will not dash my pen through it.

Let me, however, make sail and get under way with my yarn.

Cast we our eyes outward once again, beyond the boats with their beautiful coxswains—I mean *hen*-swains—to where that huge glistening iron mass floats proudly on the main. Reader, that object is the heroine, if I may so say, of this very unromantic story. She is in strange contrast with the numerous wooden veterans around her—relics of Old England's fighting days. I thought as I gazed on that splendid ship that, had I my choice, nothing would suit me better than to go to sea in her.

A month has passed; it is the 4th of July, in the year of grace 1878, and my wish is likely to be consummated, for I find myself on this morning, with several hundreds of others, taking a short trip across the harbour to the "Iron Duke," for so is she named, corrupted by irreverent mariners into the "Irish Duke."

We skip lightly up the side, or through the ports, bundling boxes, bags, and hats unceremoniously through anywhere; and find ourselves, though not without sundry knocks and manifold bruises, standing on the quarter-deck.

With a few exceptions we are all West-countrymen, undoubted "dumplings" and "duff-eaters"—at least, so say our East-country friends, though experience has taught me, and probably many of my readers too, that at demolishing a plum pudding the east is not a whit behind the west; in that particular we all betray a common English origin.

Though our ship's company is, seemingly, young, very young, the men are growing, and lusty and strong: and bid fair, ere the end of our commission, to develope into the ideal British sailor. A stranger, perhaps, would be struck with their youthful appearance; for strangers, especially if they be midland men, have an idea that a sailor is a hairy monster, but once removed from a gorilla or a baboon; and if we accept the relationship to these candated gentry, I don't think his ideas would be far out—say a dozen years since. But these terrible monsters are all now enjoying their well-earned pensions in rural quiet, leaving to the youngsters of this generation the duty of supplying their places in that great fighting machine—the navy.

The sailor of to-day possesses, at least, one decided advantage over his brother of the past. In the olden days —not so very olden either—if one man in a ship's company could read and write a letter he was considered a genius; now a sailor is, comparatively, an educated man: and if one is to be found who cannot read and write well, and accomplish far more abstruse things with his head, he is dubbed— a donkey. He is not now the debauched ignoramus which has made the English sailor a proverb all over the world. Education is of little value if it is not capable of changing a man's habits for the better. There is, however, much room for improvement in certain national traits; *apropos* of this, the "Mail" for September, 20th, 1880, lies before me, wherein the writer, in a leading article, after giving a description of the combined squadron at Gravosa, goes on to say, "It is amusing to find that the traditional impression of an Englishman prevails so largely at Gravosa, Ragrusa, &c., namely, that he is always drunk, or has just been drunk, or is on the point of being drunk." Great, though, was the surprise of the honest Ragusans when they discovered that their estimate of that erratic creature was at variance with the testimony of their experience of him; for the writer further adds, "The conduct of our men ashore, the neat, clean appearance they present, and their orderly and *sober* behaviour has been much commented on."

But this is a digression—let me bring to the wind again. At the time of our arrival on board neither the captain nor the commander had joined. The first lieutenant was, however, awaiting us on the quarter-deck, and who, with the promptness of an old sailor, allowed no time to be wasted, but proceeded at once with the work of stationing his crew.

At length every man knows his place on the watch-bill, and we hurry off to the lower deck to look after our more private affairs.

It needs not that I enter into a long and dry description of the peculiar construction of our ship, of the guns she carries, or how she is fitted out. You yourselves are far more qualified to do that than I am. After just a cursory glance at these particulars we see about getting some "*panem*," especially as a most delectable odour from the lower regions assails our nostrils, betraying that that indispensable gentleman, the ship's cook, has lavished all his art on the production of a sailor's dinner. "Man is mortal," so we yield to the temptation, especially as we are awfully hungry —when is a sailor not so? Few meals present so much food for wonderment to the landsman as does a sailor's first dinner on board a newly-commissioned ship; all is hurry, bustle, and apparently hopeless confusion. Bags and hammocks lie about just where they ought not to lie; ditty boxes are piled anywhere, and threatening instant downfall; whilst one has to wade knee-deep through a whole sea of hats to reach a place at the tables.

A jostling, animated, good-natured throng is this multitude of seamen, intent on satisfying nature's first demand; for dinner is the only meal, properly so called, a sailor gets. Nor does it matter much, though the ship's steward has not yet issued a single utensil out of which we can dine; such a slight annoyance is not likely to inconvenience men who, in most things, are as primitive in their mode of living as were our progenitors in the garden of story. Bear in mind, the object we have in view is to clear those tables of their frugal burdens—hunks of boiled beef, absolutely nothing else. What, then, though there be no elaborate dinner service, so long as the end is attained, and that it is, and in the most satisfactory and expeditious manner, with scrupulous neatness and perfect finish, our friends from the shore must bear witness.

A few words, ere we fall to, descriptive of the lower deck, which serves us for "kitchen, parlour, and all." What an altitude between the decks! Can it be that those concerns up there are meant for the stowage of boxes and hats? And see, too, this systematic arrangement of bars, transverse and upright, is it possible they are anything naval? Their office, though, becomes apparent when we reflect that there are no hooks, as in wooden ships, for the hammocks. In this iron age we have advanced a step, and even sailors can now boast of having posts to their beds. For the rest, the tables are large and at a comfortable distance apart; the ports admit a cheerful amount of light and a wholesome supply of air; and —but there goes the pipe "to dinner," so I will pipe down.

A telegram had been received during the forenoon, announcing that the captain would join us further on in the day; and accordingly, at about 4 p.m., he arrived. A tall, rather slight made man is our future chief, upright as an arrow, and with an eye such as one sees in men born to command men. His reputation comes with him in that vague semi-mysterious manner—such news does travel—and we hear he is a strict "service" officer, and an excellent seaman—good qualities both, and such as the generality of man-of-war's men raise no objection to. Withal we are told he is "smart" meaning, of course, that there must be no shirking of duty, no infringement of the regulations with him. His reputation, I say, came with him, it stuck to him, and left with him. With the captain's arrival our first day on board came to an end.

On the 6th the commander joined. In appearance he is the direct antithesis of the captain, being stout, well knit, and of medium height—the ideal Englishman of the country gentleman type—bluff and hearty, and with a face as cheerful as the sun.

Let us now pass rapidly over the few intervening days, and start afresh from July 17th. So much energy and determination had been displayed by all hands, that long before most ships have half thought about the matter we were ready for sea. In the short space of twelve days, so far as we were concerned, we were quite capable of voyaging to the moon—given a water-way by which to reach her, especially with such a chief as "Energetic H." at the helm.

On the morning of the 17th, there being nothing further to detain us in Hamoaze, steam was got up, and ere long we were leaving, for a few years, the old and familiar "Cambridge" and "Impregnable," the one-time homes of so many amongst us; and bidding king "Billy" and his royal consort a long good bye! until Devil's Point hides from us a picture many of us were destined never to behold again.

Ere long the booming of our heavy guns, as we saluted the admiral, announced that we had dropped our anchor for the first time in the Sound.

After testing speed on the measured mile, powder and shell, and other explosives, were got on board and safely stowed, though it would appear that the engineer authorities were not satisfied with the results of the steam trial. A second trial was therefore deemed necessary, and on this occasion a sort of fête was made of it; for numbers of officials and un-officials, with their lady friends, came on board to witness the result. The day was beautifully fine, and the trip a really enjoyable one—the cruising ground lying between the Start and Fowey.

July 22nd.—The "long-expected" come at last, namely, the admiral's inspection.

There is a purely nautical proverb, or, at any rate, one which is so common amongst sailors, that it may be considered as such, which says "Live to-day live for ever;" one of those expressions which, somehow, everybody knows the meaning of, but which none seem to be able to render intelligible. Well, this idea is peculiarly applicable to admirals' visits; for if one can manage to live through such an atmosphere of bustle and worry, such rushing and tearing, such anxiety of mind, and such alacrity of movement as follows in the train of the great man, then surely existence at any other time and under any other conditions is an easy matter.

It was with peculiar feelings, then, that we received the august Sir Thomas, over our gangway. Nor were these feelings modified by the knowledge that Admiral Symonds is a thorough old "salt," a tar of the old school; and, as such, is, of course, *au fait* with the weak points in a ship's cleanliness and manœuvring. His inspection was, I believe, extremely satisfactory.

We hoped that with the departure of the admiral we should have been permitted to land earlier this evening, as a sort of reward for our late exertions, especially as we have not seen our homes and families by daylight for some considerable period. Imagine, then, our feelings when a signal was thrown out at Mount-Wise that we were to perform some evolution, which would consume all the remaining hours of light. But the little cherub on the royal truck, which, according to Dibdin, is perched at that commanding altitude, especially to look out that squalls don't happen to Jack, came to console us in the —at other times unwelcome—shape of a deluge of rain. Thus we got ashore earlier, though, as a set-off against so much happiness, wetter men.

On July 26th orders came that we were to proceed to Portsmouth, to take in our armament of torpedoes, and in a few hours the Start was growing small astern as we took our way up channel. We were only a night at sea, but that a dirty one—not rough, but foggy—such as one usually encounters in this great commercial highway. Early on the following morning the Isle of Wight lay abeam, and the view from the sea was most lovely: the white cliffs of the island, packed in layers like slices of cake, presenting a learned page out of the book of nature to the curious. In passing Sandown Bay we caught a distant view of the operations for raising the "Eurydice." Our thoughts naturally took a melancholy turn, for many of us had lost comrades—some few, friends—in that ill-fated ship. But I think one of the leading characteristics of the sailor is the ease with which he throws off melancholy at will. The fact is, he encounters danger so frequently, and in so many varied shapes and forms, that if he put on depressing thoughts every time he is brought face to face with it, then he would be for ever clothed in that garb.

With a pausing tribute to the dead, and many a silent prayer, perhaps—for sailors can and do pray—we steamed into Spithead, forgetting, in all probability, the Eurydice and all connected with her.

As our torpedoes were all ready for us, it was not long before they were on board and fitted in their places. Our ship was not originally intended to carry these murderous weapons, so it was necessary to pierce ports in her sides, two forward and two aft. that they may be discharged. The staff of the torpedo school brought with them twelve of these novel fighting machines, at a cost of about £300 each, though £500 is the price paid to Whitehead's firm at Fiume; but as the English Government has the authority, with certain limitations, themselves to manufacture the torpedo, they cost England the former price.

After a short trial of the discharging gear outside the circular forts we shook hands with the land of smoked haddock and sour bread, and trimmed sails for the west, reaching the Sound by the following morning, when coaling lighters attached themselves to us before you could say Jack Robinson.

Work is again the order of the day; for coaling a large iron-clad over all means some exertion I can assure you. It is most unpleasant work, nevertheless it has to be done, so we set to work with a will. Dirty as the ship was, and dirty as we all were, from the copious showers of diamond dust falling everywhere, yet nothing could daunt our friends from paying us the usual dinner-hour visit.

It was a curious spectacle to witness that farewell visit, to see coal begrimed men coming up from below, reeking with sweat, to clasp the fair hand of a mother, to snatch a kiss from the soft cheek of a sister or sweetheart, or to feel the lingering embrace of a wife.

> " Then the rough seamen's hands they wring ;
> And some, o'erpowered with bursting feeling,
> Their arms around them wildly fling,
> While tears down many a cheek are stealing."

CHAPTER II.

"Now we must leave our fatherland,
And wander far o'er ocean's foam."

GOOD BYE TO ALBION! SOUTHWARD HO! GIBRALTAR.

FAREWELL, farewell! The last words have been said! How we would have put off that last hour; how we would have blotted it out, if, by so doing, we might have avoided that farewell. I never before realised how impressive a sailor's parting is. Was it really but a few hours since that loving, clinging hands rested within our own, that we heard the scarcely breathed words which still linger in our ears? How like a dream it all seems, and how like a dream it must continue to be, until we shall once more hear those voices and feel those hands.

Thus felt we as on the morn of August, 4th, 1878, just one month from the hoisting of the pennant, we rounded the western end of Plymouth Breakwater, *en route* for the land of the Celestials. It was Sunday, and never Sabbath broke fairer than that one, or sun shone more auspiciously on the commencement of a voyage.

Our friends, I doubt not, are casting longing and tear-bedimmed eyes after us; and many a handkerchief flutters its good bye long after objects on the shore have ceased to be distinguishable. Let us leave them to their tears; for us the sterner realities of life. We are not going away for ever, I trust; and England's sailors are patriots enough to feel that their own land, and mothers, wives, and sisters are the dearest and best in the world. With a short silent prayer, commending them to God's protection, we take a last look for good and all, at old Rame Head, and endeavour if we can to banish melancholy.

But are we really at sea? for the ship is so steady, and the water so smooth, that, without the sense of sight, we have no perception of motion. Sea voyages are, as a rule, uneventful and monotonous—to the seaman, at any rate, and ours was no exception.

A few days after leaving Plymouth we were fairly in the bay so dreaded by ancient mariners, and which is popularly supposed to be for ever

"Upheaving, downrolling tumultuously."

Many a yarn have I heard old salts spin of this special and favourite abode of the god of storms: how that the seas were so high that in the valleys between the wind was taken completely out of a ship's sails; then, fearful lest each successive wave would engulf her, her trembling crew see her up-borne with terrible force, and once more subject to the full fury of the blast: how that no bottom was to be reached by the heaviest of leads and the longest of lines,—and such-like awe-inspiring wonders; or, as that most observant of naval poets, old Falconer, graphically puts it—

> "Now quivering o'er the topmast wave she rides,
> Whilst beneath the enormous gulf divides.
> Now launching headlong down the horrid vale,
> Becalmed, she hears no more the howling gale;
> Till up the dreadful height again she flies,
> Trembling beneath the current of the skies."

We probably crossed Biscay during the time the presiding restless spirit was taking holiday or sleeping; for a lake could not possibly have presented a smoother surface. Shoals of porpoises, trying their rate of speed under our bows; the dull flop of a solitary sea-bird astern, seeking sundry bits of biscuit or other waste; and the everlasting rythm of the engines were the only occurrences to mar the sameness of this part of our voyage.

Internally all the activity usually displayed on board a British man-of-war was being carried on incessantly; nothing was neglected, and the captain soon led us to see that "thorough" was his motto, and that for him there were to be no half measures. Nor did he, during the time he was with us, ever require of us more than he was ready to undertake himself. He set us such an example of zeal and activity, that though we might not altogether have approved, yet we were bound to admire it.

It is the fourth day of our voyage, and we are in sight of the high land of the Torres Vedras, at the mouth of the Tagus. Far, far away in the background, like a magnificent panorama, rise the high, time-worn summits of the Sierras of Spain. On approaching near enough to distinguish objects we discovered several large baronial castles, or convents, perched high up on bold pinnacled crags, in positions most inaccessible and impregnable. One goes back, in fancy, to the feudal days, and recalls those heroes of our boyish imaginations to the times when

"Knights were bold and barons held their sway,"

with all the consequent ills of that system of government.

Our sails are filled with the balmy breath of Portugal's orange groves as we continue our southward way. Cape St. Vincent soon rises, Dungeness-like, right ahead, and we call to mind that this was the scene of one of England's great naval victories. These rocks, so still and peaceful now, have resounded to the din of deadly strife, when, in the year 1797, a Spanish fleet, of twenty-seven sail, tried to wrest the dominion of the seas from its lawful holders, the English fleet, under Sir John Jervis, numbering only half that of the enemy.

Next, never to be forgotten Trafalgar is reached. Trafalgar, glorious Trafalgar! a household word so long as England shall endure. How our thoughts love to dwell on the deeds you witnessed our fathers do, every man of whom was a hero.

And now arrives Sunday, August 11th, on which day, after having been favoured with exceptionally fair weather, Gibraltar, with its mighty rocky fortress, heaves in sight.

Before we arrive at the anchorage I would beg a slight indulgence of my readers whilst I twist a yarn about "Gib.;" and as, I think, much of the interest attaching to a place or object is due to a knowledge of its previous history, I purpose to give just a rapid and cursory glance at a few of the leading events connected with the past of the places we visit.

Gibraltar is of Moorish origin, having been named after the famous Saracen chieftain, Tarik, who made this rock the starting point of his conquests in Spain. Hence it was called Gib-el-Tarik—the hill of Tarik—further Europeanized into the modern Gibraltar. This magnificent natural fortress rises perpendicularly to a height of 1300 feet from the purple waves of the Mediterranean. It and the peak Abyla, on the opposite (African) coast, were styled by the Greeks, in their poetical language, "the pillars of Hercules;" whilst the strait between is said to have been executed by the same man of muscle, to wile away the tedium of an idle hour.

The remnants of this now almost-forgotten race—the Saracen—are still to be found on the northern seaboard of Africa, in the kingdom called Morocco, where they strive to eke out a scant existence from the arid plains of that parched and burning clime.

The events I have recorded above happened hundreds of years ago. Let us leap the gulf of time, and see if there be anything else worthy of note or interest as bearing upon Gibraltar. I think there is—much that is interesting to Englishmen. In 1704, Sir George Rooke and Admiral Byng had made several attempts to engage the French fleet, but had signally failed. Deeming it undesirable to return to Plymouth in this inglorious manner, the two leaders determined to win laurels for themselves and fleet somehow and somewhere—it mattered not where, and they decided on making a bold attempt on Gibraltar.

It was during this memorable attack that the signal gallantry of the Royal Marines displayed itself in so brilliant and wonderful a manner—gallantry which has shed such lustre on the annals of naval warfare, and gained for them a name and a place second to none in the British army.

In 1713, on peace being proclaimed, the fortress was ceded to England in perpetuity; but the Spaniards had no intention of abiding by a treaty wrung from them at such a cost. The result was that several subsequent attempts were made to regain the place. At length, in the years 1789-93, occurred that memorable siege—the greatest, perhaps, on record—when a mere handful of British soldiers, under General Elliott, successfully withstood a siege of three years' duration, which settled at once and, let us hope, for ever the question as to who were henceforth to be masters here. But it is a bitter pill to the Spaniards; and even now they can scarcely realize that it does not belong to them. The Spanish people are continually being buoyed up with the pleasant fiction, that it is only *lent* to its present proprietors; for in all documents relating to Gibraltar, or in all questions raised in the Spanish parliament touching that place, the British are referred to as being only "*in temporary possession of Gibraltar.*"

The view of the town from the bay is rather pleasing. Before us and far away to the left, till hid by an eminence, the houses stand out boldly, terrace above terrace, against the rocky background—their white mass and gaily-colored verandahs glistening in the sunbeams.

B

To prevent loss of time, instead of anchoring we were at once secured alongside the jetty, thus offering a fine opportunity for sight-seers, who speedily throng the wharf. A most motley gathering that same crowd, a few were undoubtedly British, therefore nothing need be said of them—a few more, half-blooded Spaniards; and as we shall become better acquainted on our visiting the town, we will pass them without comment also; but one remarkable race, which has its representatives amongst the sea of faces before us, needs a few words of remark. Their proud, commanding bearing, clearly-cut features—as if just from the sculptor's chisel, their sallow complexion—almost approaching a saffron hue, all are new to us. Red fez caps on a close-shaven head, loose flowing scarlet tunics, bare legs, and sandalled feet—these clearly betray their oriental origin. Who are they? Reader, a few pages back I endeavoured to claim your interest in a people who once owned half Spain—the Moors: these before you are some of their descendants, and are a portion of the army of the Sultan of Morocco, here for the purpose of receiving instruction in gunnery. Though they have such proud looks they are extremely bashful and restive under our gaze, constantly shifting their position to escape our scrutiny; as for making a sketch of one, that is nearly impossible, for immediately he sees you put your pencil to paper he vanishes in the crowd, as though he had detected you levelling a revolver at him.

The other dwellers on the soil are a strange mixture of the Mediterranean race; and as it is impossible to describe them, or say what they are, we will just be content with the title they are proudest of—the reptilian one of "rock scorpions"—a tough, hardy people, though, notwithstanding their doubtful ancestry.

In my description of places I shall always assume that about twenty or thirty of my shipmates accompany me in my strolls,—we shall get along much pleasanter, and enjoy ourselves much better thus than if we were scattered without any end in view: besides, it will be much less difficult for me, and I shall be enabled to get rid of that objectionable personal pronoun, first person singular, nominative. I will, therefore, with your kind co-operation, introduce you to the first of our series of rambles.

The climate is beautiful and the air most exhilirating, two, at any rate, of the attributes to an enjoyable walk already manufactured for us. Passing out of the Dockyard precincts we are at once in the English quarter. As I said before, the houses are constructed in terraces: hence we find ourselves continually mounting flights of steps to get from one street to another, so that there is really little inducement for pedestrians to move out of doors at all. Vegetation is very scarce, a want we can scarcely be surprised at when we consider the soil. Of course, that camel of the vegetable world, the cactus tribe, has its representatives in this arid, parched earth, where, seemingly, it is impossible anything else can take root.

As we approach the rising ground, which hides a portion of the town from our view, we observe the walls of an old ruin boldly outlined against the pure blue of the sky. This is all that now remains of a Moorish castle, the last existing monument of that race in Gibraltar.

But we must hurry on, for we have a lot to do: amongst other things, a climb to where that flag flutters indistinctly in the breeze. After sundry twists and turns, now up these steps, now down this street, or that, we find ourselves at the beginning of the ascent, and in as rubbly and dusty a pathway as one would wish to traverse. What with the ruts worn by the rain, and the tearing up of the ground by the passage of heavy ordnance, it would be a difficult matter indeed to select any particular line of march and call it a road. Travellers ordinarily engage mules for the journey; we sailors scorn any such four-footed assistance, though the next time we voyage this way it will be as well to remember that ankle boots are preferable to "pursers' crabs." As we advance, the sun's rays are beginning to get unpleasantly warm, whilst the sand most persistently ignores all the known laws of gravity, by fixing itself in our eyes, mouths, and nostrils.

Herds of goats, with their attendant shepherds, occasionally cross our path, changing their pasturage. Query, what do they live on? I don't think that any of our party have yet seen anything green since we started, not a blade of grass nor even a moss to relieve the stony reality of the hard rock.

With what a sigh of relief and satisfaction we reach the top, and enter within the welcome shade afforded by the signal-house. Refreshments are eagerly sought after, anything to wash the dust out of one's mouth. There is no lack of drinks here, very fortunately; beer aud stout, and something—which being put into lemonade bottles passes, I suppose, for that beverage—are speedily, greedily, gulped down our parched throats. The supposed lemonade which, by special desire, fell to my lot, was enough to engender thoughts of disloyalty to a certain lady and her cause in the mind of the stoutest champion of the league; and I took considerable credit to myself that I passed scathless through such a trying ordeal. What stuff! Just imagine, you who are drinking your stout with such keen relish, and smacking your lips in such evident satisfaction, imbibing a liquid as hot almost as the surrounding air, and so insipid that I have tasted medicines far more palatable. Opportunely I call to mind a proverb of our Spanish friends yonder, "The sailor who would caulk his boat must not turn up his nose at pitch;" and as, figuratively speaking, I want to caulk mine, I make a virtue of necessity, and the obnoxious liquid vanishes.

Having regaled ourselves at a very moderate cost, all things considered, we are are invited to insert our names in the visitors' book. To satisfy a curiosity we possess we turn back over the pages, to see who has honored this height with their presence. We find princes from Germany, grandees from Spain, professors from America, naval officers of almost all nations, and ladies not a few. One person of a witty and poetical turn thus records his and his friends' visit :—

"April 17th, 1878.

> Three friends this day
> Walked all the way
> To the signal station;
> There was W. T.,
> With his chum, C. G.,
> And R. H. of the British nation."

After such an enjoyable rest, suppose we just step outside on the terrace, and have a look around whilst we "do" our tobacco.

We are at a height of 1255 feet above the level of the sea; and the fatigue of the ascent is more than compensated by the view of the splendid natural panorama, spread out like a map around us. The bay of Gibraltar, with the houses of the town of Algeciras, are distinctly visible; so, too, is the southern range of the Ronda mountains, the purple Mediterranean, with the immense jumble of Afric's sparkling shores, the Atlas mountains, the Neutral ground, and the Spanish lines. These are some of the objects which never tire the eye. The precipices below us are amazingly steep, in some cases the heights even overhang. Many precious lives were lost through inadvertent steps during the first occupation; and this suggests to me a story I have read somewhere, and which I will ask your pardon for telling you.

A young officer of the garrison, who with a brother officer was on guard one day, suddenly missed his companion; and on retracing his steps a little he saw his poor friend's mangled body about 400 feet below. The sub, however, made no reference or allusion to this accident in his report. His commanding officer, on being informed of the sad business, immediately summoned his subordinate before him, and demanded an explanation of his conduct, the following dialogue taking place between them:—"You say, sir, in your report, 'N.B.—nothing extraordinary since guard mounting,' when your brother officer, who was on guard with you, has fallen over a precipice 400 feet high and been killed! call you this nothing?" Our sub, who hailed from 'auld reekie,' thus replied, "Weel, sir, I dinna think there is onything extraordinary in that; had he fa'n doon a precipice 400 feet high, and *no!* been killed, I should ha'e thocht it vera extraordinary indeed, and would ha'e put it doon in my report!"

I think we have found the down journey not nearly so difficult or wearying as the ascent, for we are in the town ere we are aware of it, and following in the wake of a throng of people, seemingly all heading in one direction. As we have still a few hours left us we will accompany them, and make a study of Spanish life by gaslight.

Graceful, black-eyed women, instinct with loveliness and vivacity, claim our first notice—first, because they are ladies, and, secondly, because of their becoming attire and the natural grace of their movements; for theirs is "the very poetry of motion." We have all possibly seen pictures of Spanish women, and may have, no doubt, remarked the head-gear they were depicted with. The flowing lace adornment, reaching from the head to the shoulders, and from thence thrown in graceful folds over the back and one arm, is called the "mantilla," and is the characteristic costume of the ladies of Spain. Each carries a fan in her hand—no lady is dressed without it—which they use, not so much for the purpose of cooling themselves as to convey the subtle emotions of the Spanish female mind. It seems to do the duty of eyes, though they possess very beautiful eyes, too. What I mean is, that whereas we in our colder climate generally indicate love, passion, or melancholy by means of the eyes principally, and through the facial muscles generally, these ladies interpret all this through the agency of the fan. So skilled are they in its use, that there is scarcely an emotion, it is said, which they cannot render intelligible by this means.

To say that we passed them without an impertinent stare is to confess at once that we are not sailors. This want of manners, or seeming want, is excusable, I think, insomuch that in our everyday life we see so little of them, that when we do fall across "the sex" we regard them more in the light of curiosities than tangible flesh and blood like ourselves. I see, too, that some of the more susceptible of our party are looking behind them. "Remember Lot's wife," and remember, too, the blue-eyed girls of your village homes whom you parted from so recently; for the Spanish maids, with all their charms, will scarcely bear comparison with our bonnie English lasses.

We have said something of the "*senoras*," now a word for the "*senors*." The dress of the men is as picturesque and gaudy as that of the ladies is not; in the particular, indeed, the sexes seem to have usurped the other's rights. Young Spanish swells, in colored velvet breeches and tastefully embroidered leggings, scarlet silk sash around the loins, and irreproachable linen, with, here and there, one with the far-famed guitar, improvising amorous nothings for the ear of some susceptible damsel, abandon themselves to the luxury of the hour in true Spanish style.

But what is this? Whither has the crowd conducted us? Surely the fairies have been at work! In other words, we have wandered into the Alameda, or Public Gardens. I beg to recall a statement which I fear I made somewhat rashly a few pages back, in which I said that Gibraltar could not possibly yield any green thing, owing to its miserable soil. I find I am wrong, for here before us is a perfect greenery. Stately trees, beautiful blossoms, fragrant and gaily-flowered shrubs, ferns and grasses—all are here in abundance. How charming it all looked by the light of many colored lamps! These gardens are evidently the favorite promenade of all classes of the people—the Spanish don, the English officer, the Southern Jew, and the swarthy African—all find a place in its walks, and glide along its various avenues in twos or threes, according to taste. The strains of the Garrison band, too, invite us to linger yet, as the sweet airs of the reminiscences of Scotland whisper among the branches. Sombre-clad priests, in long togas and shovel hats, bustle about here and there, now talking cheerfully to one lady, now looking correction at another; but all enjoying themselves with as much evident pleasure as their more mundane flocks.

The boom of the Citadel gun cuts short all our pleasing reflections, and we may (very unwillingly it must be confessed) tear ourselves away from this happy place.

On arriving at the Dockyard gates we are summoned to give the pass-word by the vigilant guard before we are allowed to pass the ponderous portal. Those who have read Captain Marryatt's delightful story, "Peter Simple," and I should hope there are few sailors who have not, will perhaps recall the amusing scene which took place on this very spot between lieutenant O'Brien and the soldier on guard.

Our days at pleasant "Gib." are drawing to a close. I feel assured that we shall carry with us, in our voyage to the far east, many pleasing recollections of Gibraltar—its balmy air and genial climate—its abundance of grapes, melons, and oranges. Would we could send some to our friends in England.

CHAPTER III.

*Melita ! The glory of a triumph clings, odorous as incense,
Around thy hero dead !*

UP THE MEDITERRANEAN.—MALTA.

WITH the dawn of August 15th we were rounding Europa Point, and leaving Gibraltar far away astern. On our starboard hand three or four luminous points in the atmosphere indicate the position of the snow peaks of Atlas, the range itself being lost in the distance.

We chanced on a favoring breeze, so all sail was spread to help us against the strong five knot current always setting out from this sea. I cannot tell with what feelings you entered upon this, the greatest highway of commerce in the world. For all of us it possesses a certain interest, but to some more so than to others. I refer to those who love to wander in imagination amidst the departed glories of Greece and Rome—empires which lived, moved, and had their being when our forefathers were but tattooed savages.

As we advance, the sea begins to widen, the mountainous outline of the Spanish coast trends boldly to the northward; whilst the African shore grows indistinct and flatter, save where here and there some mighty peak rears its head from out of cloudland. Since leaving "Gib." we have been under the escort of shoals of porpoises, who ever and anon shoot ahead to compare rate of speed; or, by way of change in the programme, to exhibit their fishy feats under the ship's bows. Whether there be any truth in the mariners' yarn, that the presence of porpoises generally indicates a change in the wind, I will leave for you to form your own opinion; but certain it was, that on the present occasion, the wind did change, and to a "muzzler" illustrating in the most practical manner that our ship could be just as lively on occasion as other pieces of naval architecture. The stomachs of some of our younger hands, too, seemed to have suddenly acquired a sympathetic feeling with the movements of the ship, which, strangely enough, impressed them with a desire to reveal what they had had for dinner. The ship, though, dashed onward like a mad thing, regardless of the agony she was inflicting on some of her human parasites.

This was but the commencement of our sufferings for now the heat was beginning to annoy us. To us who could go on deck when we wished it was bad enough, but to those poor fellows who had to swelter and toil in the stokehole it must have been very trying, though compared with what was yet to come this was a mere bagatelle. We had encountered that blasting wind known as the "sirocco"—the scourge of the Mediterranean—which after gathering force and heat in the African deserts comes with its fiery and sand-laden breath to sap the moisture from all who have not the natures of salamanders. Fortunately we soon passed beyond its sphere of action.

Darkness rapidly sets in in these regions of eternal summer. The sunny shores and genial climes of the Mediterranean, where the very touch of the air seems a perfumed caress, lack only one thing to make them a paradise. Those pleasant hours which obtain in our less favoured land after the sun has set, and which we call twilight, are entirely unknown here, hours which England's youths and maidens generally appropriate to themselves, and which, in after years, recall some of the sweetest memories of their lives. Fancy a day deprived of such hours! No sooner has Phœbus veiled his glorious beams than there is a general demand for candles, and we find our liberal supply of two 'dips' a very inadequate apology for about four hours' illuminating purposes on a draughty deck.

But we must haste on our way past the Tunisian Coast, past Galita, onward through fleets of lateen rigged piratical looking crafts, with snowy sails and bird-like movements, dashing their white wings in the surge. We must not dwell too long on this peaceful and pleasant shore, for Pontellaria—an island of more interest in one sense—begins to rise ahead. This, in all probability, is the "Calypso's Isle" of the classics, but now the less poetical "Botany Bay" of the Italians. I should think that a few years' compulsory residence here is a thing to be desired rather than not, for it is a delightful spot enough, a sort of embryo continent, and nature seems to have achieved here some of her grandest works in the smallest possible space and with the least possible amount of material. As we near its shore we catch a glimpse of a pure white town, gracefully reclining on the slopes of a hill at the head of a perfect miniature of a bay. Artistically the effect is very pleasing, the glistening white houses seem as if embowered in the darkest of green foliage, each roof, each angle standing out most distinctly. Much as we regret it we see charming Pantellaria vanishing astern, for our engines will not cease their everlasting plunges to satisfy any weaknesses of ours.

How wonderfully strange and new everything seems to us; the sea, the land, its peoples, all so different to England; even the very heavens shed milder lights, have purer depths of colour. At night the stars shine out larger and with greater brilliance than we are wont to see them. Our old friend, the Great Bear, still remains true to us, though he keeps shorter watches in our southward way, others less loyal, forsake us altogether, yet in exchange if we get new forms they are not less beautiful.

Brilliant as are the skies the sea is equally so, for there seem as many gems beneath as above us; we appear to be cleaving our way through a yielding mass of liquid gold. Every dash the ship makes she seems to set the sea on fire, throwing starry sprays far over our heads on to the deck where the drops still retain their light.

At early morning on August 22nd, a great jabbering outside the ship, as though a colony of monkeys had encountered another babel, announced that we were at Malta. Boats by the hundred swarm around us, and never was seen such a gesticulating, swearing crowd, as their occupants, nor such pushing and hauling, such splashing and wrangling, and even fighting to maintain their stations alongside. One's eyes cannot fail to be arrested by these boats, but the colouring of them is what attracts particular attention. We get here our first idea of the criental love for colour, though at Malta the idea is exaggerated, because the colours do not blend harmoniously. For instance, the same boat will be painted with emerald green, vermillion, cobalt, and chrome yellow, put on without the slightest regard to effect or harmony. The eye on the bow is universal, no waterman would dare venture from the shore without such a pilot.

These little crafts, in addition to their legitimate use, have a secondary, though very important one, that of advertising mediums, not unworthy the genius of our American cousins. To select an example here and there. One boat bearing the characteristic and truly Catholic legend " Nostra Senora di Lordes," also sets forth another legend to the effect that " Every ting ver cheap here Jack," though *what* is cheap and *where* is not so clearly indicated; on another this extraordinary piece of English, " Spose you cum my housee, have got plenty." Of these same " housees " numerous tales are told; of one in particular, where you can obtain " ebery ting " except the right. You ask for beef steak, or ham and eggs, and the master of the house, in the blandest manner and with much shrugging of the shoulders, will answer you, " Me ver sorry, hab got ebery ting but that," and ditto to your next order, he has also the sang froid to tell you on your complaining of the toughness of that succulent, that his cabbage must be tender because it has been boiling *ever since the " Caledonia " went home.* If you don't enjoy it after that, all that I can say is you are over fastidious.

But to return to the busy and noisy throng alongside. Its composition differs very little from that usually encountered by ships of war in all parts of call. The washerwomen are the undoubted masters of the situation, and carry all before them. The alacrity with which they scramble up the perpendicular side of the ship is simply astonishing. It struck me that we could not do it with greater ease, notwithstanding that we possess the advantage of unfettered extremities. In the twinkling of an eye they are below, and besieging us in our messes, holding out for our inspection greasy looking rolls of paper, purporting to set forth in English, French, Italian and Spanish, and even in Greek and Turkish, the bearers' exploits amidst the soap suds. To read the English certificates while at breakfast is highly amusing and provocative of much merriment. Here is one. The writer is one " Bill Pumpkin," H.M.S. " Ugly Mug," who states that the holder, Mary Brown (who does not know Mary the ubiquitous May), " has a strange knack of forgetting the gender of a shirt, for it not unfrequently happens that you may find her with that article of male apparel on her own ' proper person,' otherwise, he says, she is all that can be desired." The said Mary B being unable to read English—or for that matter any other language—holds up her paper in triumph. Happy, ignorant Mary!

Having squared yards with the black-eyed nymphs (all the shady side of thirty), we are next assailed with the milkmen, who not only bring their cans, but also their goats on board. When the can is run out " nanny " is milked, and sent about to look for a feed under the mess-tables, a locality she is thoroughly acquainted with from frequent experience.

Our first breakfast in Malta is over, a meal not easily to be forgotten, for fruit is plentiful and good and very cheap, and milk equally so, and cans full of the latter added to the chocolate make that nutritious beverage truly delightful, while luscious grapes supply a wholesome and refreshing dietary.

Now for a run on shore. Valetta, or la Valette, in honor of one of the most famous of the Grand Masters, the modern capital of Malta, is a fairly large place, though by no means extensive enough to be styled a City, except out of courtesy. How dingy the buildings and how dusty the pavements from the crumbling masonry. The houses are so lofty that the strip of blue sky can scarcely send its light to the bottom, whilst the upper storeys have such an affectionate leaning towards each other, that the wonder is that any mortar is capable of restraining their eagerness to fall on each other's necks. But all the houses are not like this, and the character of the masonry speedily improves on emerging from the gloomy alleys into the magnificent Strada Reale, more of a roadway than a street, for though there are many grand edifices and numerous shop fronts, yet one may walk to Floriana on the one hand, and to Civita Vecchia on the other, without turning to the right or left.

This crowded thoroughfare presents at this special time in particular a most cosmopolitan appearance, for we have dropped in at Malta during the sojourn here of the Indian Contingent, brought to Europe in anticipation of difficulties with Russia.

The Maltese themselves, though unquestionably a small race, are wiry and capable of enduring great hardships.

They are very skilful artisans, the filigree jewellery of their silversmiths, for example, is unequalled as a work of art by anything of its kind in Europe. They are splendid divers, and seem equally at home in the water as on the land; the smallest coin thrown overboard being brought to the surface in a twinkling. Whatever their original language might have been, that which they now possess is a most animated one; for they throw their spars about in a most alarming manner in emphasis of what they say, inclining one to the belief that sailors have of this people, namely—if you tie a Maltese hands he can't speak.

Just a word or two descriptive of the sexes: the men we will dismiss with a few words; they are, as I said before, below the medium height, with dark Italian faces and eyes, but otherwise not remarkable. The women are, though, or perhaps I ought to have said their appearance is. Landing in Malta for the first time, a stranger is apt to conclude that every woman he sees is either a sister of mercy or a nun. This is due, in a great measure, to their national costume, about the only national possession they can now boast of, which consists of a loose gown of rusty black and a hood-like covering over the head and shoulders, also black. This construction throws their face—a rather comely one—into deep shade, almost as sombre-looking as their dress. No doubt if they could be induced to wear the various so-called aids to nature which our ladies use to make "a good figure," the Maltese women might do as an advertisement for Worth; but under the present system of dressing well, I would guarantee to produce as shapely a structure out of a stuffed bread bag with a spun-yarn around its middle.

If a people be religious, in proportion to the number of priests and sacred edifices seen in their midst, then ought the Maltese to be pre-eminently a devout people; for it seems as if every third building is a church, and every other man one meets a priest; whilst the incessant and not always melodious clanging of bells all day long, is a constant reminder that there is no lack of opportunity for devotees.

So far as the outward appearance of the priests may be taken as the index to the man's worldly position, I should pronounce their calling anything but a lucrative one; for a more seedy-looking class is rarely to be met with. Their care-worn faces and rusty and tattered garments testifying that in Valetta, at least, the proverbial easy and jolly life of the priesthood does not prevail.

In spite of the lack of good building material, there are some very fine buildings in Malta—notably, the palace, the cathedral of San Giovanni, and the opera house. The palace has its immediate entrance from the Strada Reale, by means of an arched gateway of Oriental design, whilst iron railings extend along the whole front of the structure on either side the gate. Within is the palace square, beautifully and tastefully laid out with rare exotics and flowering trees, floral designs and fish ponds. A grand marble stairway indicates the direction we are to take to reach the interior of the pile, at the head of which is a sort of vestibule, or hall, when all further progress is barred by the presence of one of the palace functionaries. We explain our errand, said functionary demurs, pulls a long face, makes sundry excuses as to its not being the proper day and so on, whilst all the time he is making a mental calculation as to the value of the expected "tip." The workings of that man's mind are as patent as the day. An English shilling speedily smooths the wrinkles off that puckered brow as if by a miracle, and makes us the best of friends. What wonders the little medallion portrait of the Majesty of England will work, what hearts soften, what doors unlock, and what hypocrites make! With a flattering and obsequious bow our guide leads the way.

The palace was built by the Knights as their regal residence, and as everything in it has been most religiously preserved, the various rooms will present a pretty fair picture of the manner of life of these soldier priests, whose portraits adorns the walls around. To the frame of each a metal label is attached, on which is an inscription in Latin, setting forth the patronymic and virtues of the original. Some are represented in military armour with bold martial air, whilst others are depicted in the more peaceful garb of priests, or civilians, but all wear the sash and cross, peculiar to the Order, the latter symbol—known as the Maltese Cross—being found on all their coins and possessions.

Out of the portrait gallery folding doors admit us to the Parliament House, where the Government officials assemble for the conduct of State business. The four walls are enriched and adorned with wonderful specimens of needlework, testifying to the patience and skill of the knights' fair friends.

But the most interesting place of all is the armoury, a vast hall at right angles to the picture gallery, in which are weapons and arms of all sizes, workmanship, and ages;

from the light rapier and fencing helmet for friendly practice, to the two-handed sword and iron casque of thirty pounds weight, for the more deadly strife. Some highly interesting relics are here, too, the original document whereby Charles V. tendered the island to the Knights—a consumptive looking cannon with very large touch-holes and very small bores—stone shot, iron shot, lead balls, all arranged in neat designs. Suits of armour of delicate filigree work, in silver and gold, in glass cases; other suits less costly, though of equal ingenuity, ranged along the walls in erect positions, spear in hand, or leaning on a huge sword. From the size and weight of some of these suits, I opine, the Knights must have been men of large build, a medium sized suit being rather the exception than otherwise.

After a glance at the old, lumbering State carriage of Bonaparte, with its faded, gilded trappings and armorial emblazonry, we haste away to view something else.

Next in importance to the Palace, comes the Church of St. John (San Giovanni), by far the finest building in Malta. The interior is very gorgeous, with gilded vaulted roof, finely carved pulpits, rare old crimson tapestries and monumental floor, resembling one enormous heraldic shield. Beneath, lie the mouldering remains of the defunct knights, the arms of each being represented on the slabs above them, in the most delicate and accurate designs, in some cases stones more rare and costly than marble being used.

At the end of the eastern aisle is the Chapel of the Madonna, guarded by massive silver bars, saved from the rapacity of Napoleon's soldiers by the cunning and ingenuity of a priest, who, perceiving that Bony's followers had very loose ideas of mine and thine, painted the rails wood colour, and thus preserved them inviolate.

Once more in busy, bustling, Strada Reale, with its gay shops filled with a tempting display of gold and silver filigree work, corals and laces, the latter very fine specimens of needlework indeed.

Thus far, we have performed all our movements on foot, but now, as we have to go a rather long distance over very uninteresting ground, we think it more convenient to sling our legs over a horse's back, for the journey to Civita Vecchia, better known to sailors as "Chivity-Vic." This was the former capital of the island, though now, as deserted almost as Babylon, its streets overgrown with grass, its buildings crumbling ruins, and echoing to the tread of our horses' hoofs. But it is not so much to view these ruins that I have brought you here, as to visit the Catacombs, or subterranean burying grounds of the early inhabitants. These are not much compared with those at Naples, or Palermo, for instance, but to those who have seen neither the one nor the other, they will present all the charm of novelty. Though only a charnel house it is laid out with great care, in street, square, and alley, just like the abodes of men above. The bodies are mostly in a fine state of preservation, reposing in niches cut out of the dry earth, some of the tombs being double, others, again, having an additional crib for a child. It is next to impossible that organic matter can fall to decay, owing to the extreme dryness of the place, and, except that the colour has changed a little, the dead people around would have no difficulty in recognizing their own faces again if brought suddenly to life. Some of the bodies seem actually alive, a deception further borne out by their being clothed in the very garments they wore when sentient, joyful dwellers, in the city above. It is worthy of remark that, though there is but one and the same means of ingress and egress, the air is wonderfully pure, and free from any offensive odour or mustiness.

Its extreme dryness though, seems somehow to have a reciprocal effect on the palates of our party, for I hear vague murmurs of " wanting something damp," which, by-an-bye, break out into a general stampede. If there be any bye-laws in existence against hard riding, we are happily ignorant of them, nor have we the slightest sympathy with anxious mothers, whose dusky and grimy offspring are engaged at a rudimentary school for cookery in the mud of the road. Sailors, as a rule, don't note such items.

August 25th, to-day, after a rather short stay, we looked our last, for some years, on " the fair isle "—St. Paul's Melita.

CHAPTER IV.

"Yet more! the billows and the depths have more!
　High hearts and brave are gathered to thy breast;
They hear not now the booming waters roar,
　The battle thunders will not break their rest."

PORT SAID.—THE SUEZ CANAL.—VOYAGE DOWN THE RED SEA.—ADEN.

THE voyage from Malta to Port Said was accomplished without any notable event, except that the heat goes on steadily increasing.

August 31st, to-day, we made the low-lying land in the neighbourhood of Port Said, and by noon had arrived and moored off that uninteresting town. Coaling at Port Said is effected with great rapidity, for ships have to be speedily pushed on through the Canal to prevent a block, thus, by the following afternoon, we commenced our first stage of the Canal passage, under the escort of one of the Company's steam tugs, for ships of our size may not use their own engines for fear of the "wash" abrading the sandy banks.

The character of the scenery soon changes, and we seem to have an intuitive perception that we are in the land of the Pharaohs. On the one side, far as the eye can reach, and for hundreds of miles beyond, a desert of glistening sand is spread before us, for the most part level and unbroken, but occasionally interrupted by billow-like undulations, resembling the ground swell at sea. Here and there a salt pond breaks the monotonous ochre of the sand. These ponds are, in the majority of cases, quite dry, and encrusted with a beautiful crystalline whiteness resembling snow, making even the desert look interesting. On the Egyptian side, a series of gem-studded lagoons stretch away to the haze of an indistinct horizon, the mirage reproducing the green and gold of the thousand isles in the highly heated atmosphere.

By 6 p.m. we had reached the first station, or "Gare," when we brought up alongside a jetty for the night. When darkness had set in, the wild melancholy howl of the jackal was borne across the desert by the evening breeze, a sound sufficiently startling and inexplicable if you don't happen to know its origin. What these animals can find to eat in a parching desert is, and remains to me, a mystery.

On pushing on the following morning, a quail and several locusts flew on board; interesting because we are now in the region of Scripture natural history. As I was desirous of procuring a specimen of the Scriptural locust, I expressed a wish to that effect, and soon had more of them than I knew what to do with, till, in fact, I thought the Egyptian plague was about to be exemplified. I will here take occasion to thank my shipmates for their kindly and ready assistance, in helping me to furnish a cabinet with natural history specimens. Nothing living, coming within their reach, has ever escaped them; birds, insects, fish, reptiles, all have been laid as trophies before me to undergo that metamorphosis known as "bottling." I verily believe that had an elephant insinuated himself across their path, he would have found his way into my "preserves."

This was an extremely quiet day, everybody indulging a siesta under double and curtained awnings, until about 5 p.m., when bump! a dead stop, and a list to port. We are aground. But grounding on such a soft bed is not a serious affair, and by extra exertions on the part of "Robert," our tug, and a turn or two of our own screws, we were soon in deep water again. This was but the initiation ceremony; ere the termination of our commission we were destined to become passed masters in the art of bumping, as the sequel will show.

At this juncture the Canal ceases to be such, as it enters that natural watercourse—the Bitter Lakes. Herein, we are at perfect liberty to use our own engines, whereby we are speedily across their glassy surface, and entering on to the last portion of the passage. On rounding a point on the opposite side, a scene, truly Biblical, met our view—two Arab maidens tending their flocks. Perhaps they had taken advantage of the absence of man to uncover their faces; if so, they were speedily careful to rectify the error, on catching sight of such terrible beings as bluejackets; but not before we had caught a glimpse at a rather pleasing face, with small, straight nose, rosy lips, splendid teeth, the blackest of eyes, and the brownest of skin. The veils, which serve to hide their prettiness, are real works of art, composed of gold and silver coins, beads and shells, tastefully and geometrically arranged on a groundwork of black lace. After repeated hand kissing from our amorous tars—an action whose significance is apparently lost on these damsels—we bid good bye to the "nut-brown maids," and at 5 p.m., on September 4th, enter the broad waters of the Gulf of Suez.

The great feature of the town of Suez is its donkeys; wonderfully knowing creatures, who, with their masters, look upon every visitor, as in duty bound, to engage their services. To say them nay, and to suggest that your legs are quite capable of bearing you to the town, is only provocative of an incredulous smile, or a negative shake of the head. Never was seen such patience and importunity as that displayed by boy and beast. The most striking thing about them is their names—shared in common—which furnish one with a running commentary on current events in Europe. For example, there were the "Prince of Wales" and "Roger Tichborne," "Mrs. Besant" and the "Fruits of Philosophy"! The "mokes" are so well trained—or is it that they have traversed the same ground so often? that, in spite of all tugging at the reins, and the administration of thundering applications of your heel in the abdominal region, they will insist upon conducting you to a locality well understood, but of no very pronounced respectability. I did hear—but this between you and I—that a rather too confiding naval chaplain, on one occasion, trusted himself to the guidance of one of these perfidious beasts, and even the sanctity of his cloth, could not save him from the same fate.

September 7th. We may now be said to have entered upon the saddest and most unpleasant part of the voyage, that of the Red Sea passage.

The day after sailing, the look-out from the mast head reported a vessel aground off the starboard bow, with a second vessel close by, and, seemingly, in a similar predicament. Our thoughts at once adverted to the two troopships which left last night, so we hurried on, and, arriving at the spot, found we had surmised correctly. One only, the steamer, was aground; her consort, the sailing ship, being at anchor a safe distance off. We lost no time in sending hawsers on board, but it was not until the third day that we were successful in our efforts to haul her off.

Our voyage resumed, we had scarcely got out of sight of the two ships, when the sudden cry of "man overboard!" was heard above the din of flapping canvas and creaking blocks. To stop the engines, gather in the upper sails, let fly sheets, and back the main yard, was the work of seconds; and before the ship was well around—smart as she was on her heel, too—the life-boat was half-way on her errand of mercy. Young Moxey was soon amongst us again, none the worse for his involuntary immersion, although his bath was more than an ordinary risky one, owing to the proximity of sharks.

From that exalted observatory, the mast head, we noticed the red colour from which the sea derives its name. The surface has not a general ruddy tinge, as we most of us thought it had,—only here and there blood-red patches appear, mottling the vivid blue surface.

September 11th.—My "journal" is a blank for three

whole days, owing to the intense heat, which is simply unbearable. I can only give our friends a faint idea of what it was like, by asking them to imagine themselves strapped down over a heated oven whilst somebody has built a fire on top of them, to ensure a judicious "browning" on both sides alike. Sleep is out of the question, "prickly heat" is careful of that. As may be supposed, the sufferings of the deck hands—bad enough as in all conscience it was—were not to be compared with the tortures endured by the poor fellows in the stoke-hole, who had to be hoisted up in buckets that they might gasp in the scarcely less hot air on deck. From bad, this state of things came to worse—men succumbed to its influence, the sick list swelled, and, finally, death stalked insidiously in our midst.

September 13th.—The first victim was John Bayley, a marine, who died to-day after an illness of only a few short hours. One curious thing about this sickness is that those attacked by it exhibit, more or less, symptoms of madness. One of my own messmates, for instance, whose life was preserved by a miracle, almost went entirely out of his mind. I will not dwell too long upon these sufferings, nor rekindle the harrowing scenes in your minds.

At sunset on the 14th the bell tolled for a funeral, as, with half-masted flag, and officers and men assembled, we prepared to do the last that ever poor Bayley would require from man. Funerals are solemn things at any time, but a funeral at sea is more than this—it is impressive and awe-inspiring, especially if there be others so near death's door that one does not know whose turn it may be next.

Decently and in order the hammock-clad form is brought to the gangway, whilst the chaplain's voice, clear and distinct—more distinct than ordinary it seems—reads the beautiful service for the Church of England's dead. A hollow plunge, a few eddying circles, at the words—"we commit his body to the deep"—and he is gone for ever.

Almost simultaneously with departure of one, another of our shipmates, Mr. Easton, the gunner, died.

Providentially for all of us, a squall of wind struck us at this point of our voyage—a squall of such violence, whilst it lasted, that the air was thoroughly purged of its baneful qualities, and restored again to its elasticity.

But what a God-send it was! The iron hull of our ship, always unpleasantly hot in these latitudes, was rapidly cooled by the deluge of rain which came with the wind. Renewed life and vigour entered into our emaciated frames, and revivified men marked for death; and was it not delicious to rush about naked in the puddles of rain on the upper deck!

Well, all things mundane have an end, even the most unpleasant—though it must be confessed their finality is generally lingering. Thus our desolate voyage through that seething cauldron, known to geographers and school-boys as the Red Sea, at length approached its termination.

Our grim shipmate, death, did not go over the side till he had marked yet another victim for his insatiate grasp; for, to-day, Mr. Scoble, one of our engineers, died. He, too, was buried at sea, though we were only a few hours from port. On the morn of this day, September 17th, we passed the strait of Bab-el-mandeb—Arabic for "Gate of Tears"—an extremely appropriate name, too, I should think.

Aden, which we reached the same evening, has a very bleak and barren appearance, and is, seemingly, nothing better than a volcanic rock. Its apparent sterility does not, as a matter of fact, exist; for it produces an abundance of vegetables of all kinds, splendid corn with stalks above the ordinary height, fruits, roses, and other delightful and highly-scented flowers, in rank abundance. There is something thriving and go-a-head about the place, in spite of unkindly nature. It has one terrible drawback, for rain falls only at intervals of years, sometimes taking a holiday for three or even more years. The people are busy and bustling—troops of camels, donkeys, and ostriches continually stream in and out the town, testifying to an extensive trade with the neighbouring states. A peculiar race of people is found here, the Soumali—tall, gaunt-looking fellows, with a mass of moppy hair dyed a brilliant red. This head-gear, surmounting a small black face, is laughable in the extreme. Plenty of ostrich feathers may be obtained of the Arabian Jews; and though, of course, you pay sailors' prices for them, yet even then the sums given are not nearly so much as would be charged in England for a far inferior feather.

On the eve of departure we were visited by a novel shower, composed of sand and locusts, from the African desert. These things, unpleasant as they seem to us, are, we are told, of as common occurrence here as rain showers at home.

CHAPTER V.

"As slow our ship her foamy track
Against the wind was cleaving,
Her trembling pennant still look'd back
To that dear isle 'twas leaving."

ACROSS THE INDIAN OCEAN.— CEYLON.— SINGAPORE.— A CRUISE IN THE STRAITS OF MALACCA.

SEPTEMBER 21st.—Having, as it were, given the go-by to two continents, we commence on an extended acquaintance with a third.

With sails spread to a S.W. monsoon we rapidly speed over that glorious expanse of luminous sea where it is ever summer, and in whose pearly depths living things innumerable revel in the very joy of existence.

Though hot, this part of the voyage is not unpleasant, for a cooling breeze is constantly setting down the hatchways from the sails. What one would rather be without, though, is that tropical tinting known as the "prickly heat," which now begins to get troublesome; for, like boils, its spots generally select those parts of the epidermis where they are likely to become of the greatest nuisance, making the friction of garments almost intolerable; but there, one can't have everything.

When the sails are trimmed with the same regularity day after day, with never a tack nor sheet started, existence does not offer much of variety, so that, like Columbus' sailors, we were glad to welcome even a gale of wind. Now, a rolling and pitching ship is capital fun if you can manage to stay the surgings of a revolutionary stomach; but it sometimes happens that you can't, when, to vary a line in "In Memoriam," "you heave responsive to the heaving deep." Then, too, we [are as hungry as "sea dogs." Ten or twelve days on sea rations are not to be envied, especially as there is plenty of room for improvement in the dietary. It is all very nice, nay, pleasant even, to feel hungry when there is a prospect of a good "feed" in the tin dish; but how frequently do we find a "southerly wind" prevailing in that receptacle for "panem;" and what is there, I ask, in "Fanny Adams" alternated with "salt junk?" In the one, nausea; in the other, mahogany.

Friday, October 14th.—Just at our breakfast hour we sighted that oriental fairy garden, Ceylon's isle; and though we must be from fifteen to twenty miles off, a curiously-constructed native vessel, with perhaps a dozen persons on board, has just put out to welcome and pilot us to land. A boat so different to all other boats that I must say a word about it. It is a sort of double canoe, constructed of the hollowed out trunk of a cocoanut tree, to which is attached a couple of outriggers, with a second canoe-shaped structure at their extremities, but of lesser dimensions than the boat proper, and differing from it, too, in not being hollowed out—in fact the latter is used only as a balance for the other. When it comes on to blow with any force, the Singalese boatmen may be observed standing out on their outriggers, to counteract the force of the wind on the high sails. The stronger the breeze the further out the men go. Their mode of expressing the intensity of a breeze is significant. The Singalese don't say as we do, it is blowing stiff, or half a gale, or a gale; but that it is a "one-man wind," or "two," or "three-man wind," as the case may be. I believe a similar idiom is used by the natives of the Sandwich isles.

On nearing the land we could see how really delightful this ocean gem is. One mass of gorgeous, perfumed foliage blazes suddenly on the sight from the midst of the sea; feathery palms, broad trembling leaves, and groves of lofty cocoanut trees springing from the midst of richly-flowering shrubs.

From the inner harbour the view of Galle is very fine. For miles on either hand stretches a palm-fringed shore, with the noble cocoanut trees so close to the water's edge, that at times the sea seems to dash right into their midst. Cocoanut trees, like volcanoes, seemingly prefer the proximity of the sea to a more retired position.

The whole scene reminds one of the beautiful places visited by captain Cook, in his voyages. Even the boats are laden with the self-same royal fruits—great green cocoanuts, pine apples, bananas, plantains, and yams.

All those curiosities for which India is famous—every conceivable article which the fancy or ingenuity of man can possibly fabricate out of such commodities, as sandal wood, ebony, ivory, and porcupines' quills, richly and delicately carved, may be had here for a mere song if you possess only patience. Amongst other things there is a brisk trade carried on in precious stones. Some of the dealers in this article have found their way to our lower deck, and proceed to pull little parcels, containing sparkling and pellucid gems from their inner garments. There, before us, in their downy nest, lie rubies, sapphires, opals, and many more real or fictitious stones, seven-eighths of which are probably manufactured at Birmingham, though Ceylon abounds in real gems. It may, I think, be safely conceded that "Jack" very rarely drops in for one such. The dealers ask most fabulous prices for their wares—so many thousand rupees; but after haggling with you for about an hour or so are glad enough to part with them at your own price—a proof, should you need it, of the *genuineness* of your purchase.

We are rather dubious at first about entering the canoes, for they are so narrow as scarcely to admit of our broad hams being comfortably stowed. However, by dint of a little laterel pressure in that quarter, we at length manage to wedge ourselves in. We find the motion pleasant enough—a sense of security growing with experience.

I suppose we are not the first, nor, unless some sudden calamity undertake the place, are we likely to be the last, who have remarked how exceeding annoying the "boys" at the landing-place are. Guides they call themselves; sailors, in their excellently-terse and rotund way, call them by another name, which certainly does not commence with a "G." These wasps know just sufficient of English to make you disgusted with your mother tongue. The ordinary and generally conclusive argument of applying the toe of one's boot to the region of their quarter galleries does not seem to be effective here. It is one of those things one has to put up with.

The town follows the sinuous windings of the shore for upwards of a mile and a half, under an arcade of cocoa palms, which forms one of the finest promenades imaginable. Under this quivering canopy the fierce rays of the outside sun filter through—a soft, sheeny, mellow light—making his tropic rays deliciously cool, at the same time imparting to them a mystic coloring of gold and emerald green in all their wonderful combinations and capabilities of tone, impossible to set down in writing.

A noticeable thing about all this wonderful profusion, is the number of beautiful shrubs, principally spice or perfume bearing, and the grand harmonies and contrasts of colour they present. Here, for example, is the nutmeg, with its peach-like fruit; here the cinnamon, a tree whose foliage embraces the most delicate gradations of colour, from olive green to softest pink; there an aromatic gum tree, the dark-leaved coffee tree, the invaluable bread fruit, and scores of others beyond my botanical ken.

The houses, examined in detail, are not by any means the captivating objects we took them to be from the ship; and they certainly don't improve on a closer acquaintance. The air in the vicinity is thick and heavy, with a rancid odour of cocoanut oil, emanating from the hair and bodies of the local humanity. Their dwellings are constructed of humble enough materials, in all conscience; for of the four sides, three are of mud, the fourth being left open for the purposes usually supplied by doors, windows, and chimneys amongst ourselves. A sort of blind of cocoa-nut-fibre covers this aperture to about half way, so that one can easily see what is going on within. Near the door reclines an indolent, almost nude man, in the most convenient attitude for sleep; in the far corner his wife or slave—for the names are synonymous—toiling and moiling at a stone mill—a gaunt, angular, ugly woman, with great rings in her nose and ears, and on her wrists and ankles. Perfectly nude children and mangy-looking curs have all the rest of the apartment to themselves; and from the way in which they are enjoying their gambols, one may judge that for them life is not an unpleasant thing on the whole. The number of brown imps scattered about the streets, threatening to upset your every movement, speaks highly of the prolificness of Singalese matrons; and if a numerous progeny is a desirable thing, then these mammas ought to consider themselves blessed amongst women. Their general aspect, though, conveys the opposite impression.

Everybody is addicted to the vice of chewing the betel-nut, a proceeding which has the effect of dyeing the teeth and lips a brilliant crimson, and gives to this people the appearance of an universal bleeding at the mouth.

Having completed a hasty perambulation of the town we drive boldly into the undergrowth to where a strange-looking building lies half-buried in the foliage. It proves to be a Buddhist temple, an octagonal-shaped structure with a bell-like roof. As we enter within its precincts, boy priests are particularly careful to obliterate the marks of our *heathen* feet on their beautiful floor of golden sand. Inside are eight figures of the good Buddha, alternately standing and sitting, depicted with that calm, inscrutable countenance so remarkable in the image of this deity wherever this religion prevails. Before each figure is a small altar, littered with flowers, the most conspicuous blossom being the lotus lily, the symbol of this faith. Other than these devotional oblations there is little to be seen; what part in the ceremonies the priests take, or where they perform their functions, does not appear.

At the gate of the Court on our passing out, stands a bold, yellow-robed priest, with a metal salver in his hand, suggestive of donations. We told the old gent with naval bluntness that we were not in the habit of aiding the Society for the propagation of paganism—a remark, by the way, which it was as well, perhaps, he could not understand.

Sunday, October 6th.—Though sailors are excellent singers—especially of hymn tunes—I never before heard a hymn rendered so effectively on board a man-of-war as that beautiful composition by Bishop Heber, commencing

"What though the spicy breezes
Blow soft o'er Ceylon's isle,"

and which was one of the appropriate hymns for our morning Service.

October 8th.—Towards evening we bade good-bye to this favoured land, and stood away to the eastward. We had made good an offing, and set everything aloft snug for the night, when heavy volumes of steam were found to be issuing from the regions of the engine-room. A steam pipe had burst, a fracture of so little moment that after a short delay to effect repairs we were able to resume our voyage. But though the damage was not serious, so far as the ship was concerned, to us, personally, it was a matter of some consequence, on account of our bags and chests being stowed immediately over the fractured pipe; and in order to secure our property, we were compelled to make a blind rush for it, re-appearing from our vapour bath, as red as boiled lobsters.

A splendid eight knot breeze brought us, after a few days, off Acheen head, in Simatra, and at the entrance of the Straits of Malacca. And here, the monsoon which had favoured us over so many miles of the pathless ocean, suddenly forsook us. Sails were of no further use, and we braced up our sweat glands for four or five days of increasing heat. In obedience to the demands of an imperious, ever-rising, thermometer, we reduced our rig to the least possible articles consistent with decency and the regulations of the Service—which latter, by the way, discriminates not between the caloric of the north pole and that of the equator.

Just at this time, we encountered a phenomenon of frequent occurrence in this region, namely, water-spouts. One of these tremendous, funnel-shaped, columns of water actually burst just ahead of us, drenching our decks in showers of spray, and causing the water to seethe and vex itself as though some monster were lashing it into fury.

October 18th.—The scene which presented itself to our eyes, as we entered the narrow, gem-studded channel which leads up to Singapore was such that I trust it may live long in my mind as a memory picture of grateful and refreshing beauty. I don't know that it will compare with the mighty growth of Ceylon's forests, or with the variety and richness of its forms; but for mellowness of tint and harmonious blending of soft foliage, Singapore's park-like views seem to me, as yet, unrivalled. The channel is so narrow and its banks so high, that one is quite unprepared for the splendour which suddenly, like the shifting lights in a transformation scene, blazes out in all its tropic splendour. *Now*, the scenes depicted in the "Arabian Nights" seem to me not so impossible after all, and, except that gems don't grow on the trees, this fairy garden might well have stood in the writer's mind as his ideal of paradise.

Very reluctantly we turn away, as that grim reality, known as the Tangong Pagar coaling wharf, heaves in sight, and alongside which we are rapidly secured. Hundreds of coolies, in anticipation of our enormous wants—500 tons of carbon—are already thronging the jetty with their baskets of coal, which ere long, is rattling down our coal shoots.

The Malays, though labouring under the disadvantage of a bad reputation, are a well developed, muscular race, of a dark, copper colour. Dress does not trouble them much, for all that custom and society demand of them in this respect is a couple of yards or so of white linen about their lumbar region; the remainder of their sleek, oily bodies presenting the appearance of polished bronze. They are great divers, especially the youths and boys—I had almost said *infants*, for some of the little mortals can scarcely have passed the sucking age. Their stock of English is very limited: "Jack, I say jack, I dive," delivered all in one mouthful and with no regard to punctuation, being about the extent of their acquirements in our tongue.

Our first day at Singapore was marked by a sad termination. Emanuel Dewdney, one of our boys, a weakly lad and far too delicate for the rough life he had adopted, died of heat apoplexy in the afternoon.

Though Singapore lies so near the equator—within two degrees of it in fact—it enjoys a very healthy, though, of course, a very hot climate. The town itself is not very extensive. There is the usual native Malay division with its system of mud architecture, its dirt and smells; and that of the European residents—a marked contrast to the irregular jumble of the other. I don't know that there is particularly much to see in the island, except, perhaps, the Botanical Gardens, whose beauties will amply repay you for the rather long walk to reach them. You may take a coach if you like, but that will spoil the pleasure. In these gardens all the choicest and rarest flora, and much of the fauna, of the East Indies, are brought together and acclimatized. The most conspicuous amongst the former, and certainly the most lovely—and that is saying much where all excel—is a species of acacia, a large tree with great flaming scarlet and yellow flowers. Then there is that extremely interesting and singularly funny creeper, the sensitive plant, which, on the approach of anybody, has the power of doubling up its leaves as if in sudden fear. Birds in great variety—all scarlet, gold, and azure—inhabit spacious aviaries within the grounds. Lyre birds, argus pheasants, great eagles, and owls from Java, doves, pigeons, liries, and humming birds, the metallic lustre of whose plumage flashes in the light like the sheen of steel. One or two tigers—in a cage, of course—invite our curiosity. I was not, however, prepared to make quite so close an acquaintance with these lovely supple creatures, as one of the marines of our party, who, having indulged too freely in malt, possibly mistook the animals for cats, the result being he got so damaged about the bows as to be rendered unfit for divisions the following morning, and barely escaped with his eyesight. Drink makes a man do queer things.

The native men are very picturesquely apparelled in gaily coloured turbans and sarongs, whilst the women,—tall, graceful, and pretty—convey a small fortune about with them, in the shape of jewellery, in the cartilage of the nose, in the ears, and around the arms and legs. I saw one woman who had such heavy masses of gold in her ears that the lobes of those organs touched her shoulders.

November 1st.—At 9 a.m. the long-expected "Audacious" hove in sight, flying the flag of Admiral Hillyar at the main. How we already envy her fortunate crew!

November 8th, off to Penang. The pipe "up anchor" this morning was hailed with delight. Anything to change the dull monotony of the last few weeks. We started with an overcast and rainy sky, and by the next morning had reached Malacca, a small British settlement, essentially Malay, more a village than a town. It lies very low and close to the water's edge, the houses of the natives being all constructed on piles driven into the mud, and embowered in a dense framework of cocoa palms. In the distance rises the high cone-shaped peak of Ophir, now a lovely sight because of the misty covering which envelopes it to near its summit. Bananas are very plentiful; so, too, are monkeys and the canes so highly prized at home.

November 9th.—To-day, our own admiral came in, in the mail steamer, and glad are we that he has arrived, that we may be again on the move, for you know there are happier states and more comfortable, than a forcible detention in a red-hot ironclad.

Sunday, November 13th.—I see in my "journal" that I have noted what, under ordinary conditions, would call for no remark, that a lady was present at our service to-day. None but those who are banished the softening and refreshing influence of woman's society can form any idea how pleasant it is to see an English woman in this land of yellow bellies and sable skins.

November 15th.—Now we are really the Flag Ship, for this morning the "Audacious," with a parting cheer, bade us good-bye, and started for home.

November 21st.—By early morning we discovered the island of Din Ding right a-head.

Nothing can exceed the wonderful beauty of this tiny island. From the sea it has so much the appearance of the bosky slopes of Mount Edgcumbe, that, were it not for the characteristic palm, one could well imagine one's self looking at a bit of our own dear England.

A stretch of sandy beach, white and glistening as silver, with the graceful waving plumes of the cocoanut tree close to the water's edge, and behind, the pile dwellings of the Malays, nestling at the foot of a wooded eminence, capped to its very summit with a dense and varied growth; such is the picture viewed from the anchorage. Din Ding, or Ding Ding—as sailors, by a system of alliteration, very fashionable amongst themselves—render it, lies at the mouth of the Perak river.

On landing we struck at once into the jungle, under tall palms, with their great ripening fruit, and other tropic vegetation. Road, there was none; only a sort of bridle path, very heavy with mud, and overgrown with great hawser-like creepers, indicated a way along which we trudged. Now and then the fallen trunk of a great tree barred our further progress, or a chasm yawned before us, or mayhap, a great time-worn boulder stopped the way; insignificant objects all when matelôts are on the war trail. Our object was to reach a certain house on yonder point, in which a most dastardly murder was recently perpetrated on the British resident, Colonel Lloyd, who, with his wife and sister, had made this their home. The house is now quite empty, but in one of the rooms we saw, or fancied we saw, spots of sanguine dye on the floor.

We hastened onward through a small hamlet of about a dozen miserable huts, resting on piles. Tubs of putrid fish, in all stages of decomposition, gave out a most horrid stench, whilst other carcasses strewed the ground in advanced rottenness. Is it not revolting, that amongst these people, fish in its pure state is rarely eaten, and if it be, it is always raw. But nature is ever lovely, though the human part of her does all it can to deface her; if she were not so what a spoiled world ours would be!

Holding our nostrils we ran for it, doubtful if we should ever get rid of the smell. Further on was a hut of rather larger pretensions, now used as a barrack for the police. One of these latter, who possessed a tolerable knowledge of English, struck up a conversation with us, and amongst indifferent topics we asked about the prisoners recently captured. He certainly took us by surprise, when he indicated they were within the building, alongside of which we were standing. Would we like to see them? We would. Yes, true enough, there on the floor were five Chinamen, lashed and bound so tight that the flesh stood out in great purple ridges on either side the rope.

To get back to our boat we had to repass the village of odours delectable. On this occasion the scantily clad and polished Malays, whom we had not seen on passing through, put in an appearance.

By 4 p.m. the anchor was aweigh, and we heading towards Penang, which was reached on the following day in the midst of thick, dirty weather.

The town is well built, and the cleanest I have yet seen since leaving Europe. The island is sometimes termed the "Garden of the East," and if it is always as now, I should say the name was justly bestowed. A little way out in the country is a fine waterfall, which all who call here, make a point of visiting. Jumping into a pony carriage, locally called a *gharry*, a comfortable, well ventilated vehicle, capable of seating four persons, we desire the turban driver to steer for the latter place. Along the very fine road to the fall, a profusion of palms and gigantic tree ferns, between thirty and forty feet high, up whose great stems gaily flowered creepers wind their hawser-like fronds, make a delicious and cooling shade. Yonder tree away there in the background, with delicate pea-green leaves, is an old friend of ours. Let your memories go back to your infancy. Cannot you recall many a wry face; cannot you remember how unpleasant the after sensations when stern, but kind mothers forced a nauseous decoction called "senna" down your widely-gaping throat ? You smile. I felt certain you had all experienced it. Well that is the senna tree.

Large mansions lying back from the roadway, with gates and paths leading up to their entrances, and a smell of new mown hay, were most home-like and refreshing.

We should have fared much better had a more mutual understanding existed between us and our pony. That obtuse little beast, good enough at curves and tangents, after half an hour's canter, flatly refused to exert himself above a walk ; nor, though frequently encouraged by the whip, did he accelerate his movements to the end of our drive.

At the fall we had a very refreshing shower bath under a thundering cascade of water tumbling over the edge of a gorge. Near at hand, and conveniently so, too, for the priesthood, is a small shrine sacred to the Hindoo god Brahin, a diminutive edition of whom stands on a little pedestal, amidst braziers, lamps, figures with elephants' heads and human bodies, and other monstrosities. You may be certain there was a mendicant priest in attendance on his godship.

On the return voyage our hack behaved even more ungentlemanly than before, for now he most emphatically refused to budge an inch, indicating his intention of becomiug a fixture by planting his feet obliquely, like a stubborn jackass, into the ground. Human nature could scarcely be expected to tolerate such evidence of mutiny, so, jumping into the first passing carriage, we reached the town at a fairly creditable canter.

November 28th.—To-day our short stay at Penang comes to a conclusion, and a few days afterwards we are once more at Singapore.

CHAPTER VI.

> " Merrily, merrily on we sail !
> The sailor's life is gay !
> His hopes are on the favouring gale,
> And whether it freshens, or whether it fail
> He recks not, cares not, no not he ;
> For his hope is ever upon the sea."

SARAWAK.—LABUAN.—MANILLA.—HEAVY WEATHER.

DECEMBER 5th.—At 4 p.m. the anchor was hove short for our voyage to Hong Kong, by way of Manilla. As we start some days sooner than we anticipated, we had made no provision for getting our washed clothes on board, and grave fears are entertained that we shall be compelled to sail without it, for as yet there is not so much as the ghost of a washerwoman in sight. Will they, can they by any fortuitous combination of circumstances, put in an appearance before we leave ? Despair, we are off ! But surely no, it can't be ? Yes, by jove, there are boats pulling after us with all the might the rowers can command. We lie to, the proas come nearer. Hurrah ! the clothes, some wholly washed, some half-washed, and some not washed at all. Piles of fair white linen are bundled up the gangway pell-mell, Malay washerwomen bundled *out* ditto, and for payment, the revolving screws settle that in a highly satisfactory manner.

With the " Lapwing " in tow, and the gentlest of breezes filling the lighter canvas, we shape our course eastward.

December 8th.—Late in the afternoon we brought up in the roadstead of Sarawak, on the northern coast of Borneo. The place is not at all enlivening ; neither house, human being, nor boat, to indicate we are in habitable land. The town itself, the capital of a small rajahship governed by an Englishman, lies some twenty miles up a river, in the estuary of which we are anchored. The province was presented by the Sultan of Borneo, in 1843, to Sir James Brooke, uncle of the present proprietor, who, on the decease of Sir James, in 1868, succeeded to the territory.

Here the " Lapwing," after having taken the admiral up the river, parted company, whilst we continued our way along the Bornean shore.

December 12th.—We awoke to find ourselves in the midst of a labyrinth of isles most wonderful to behold, vaguely guessing which, out of so many, can be Labuan. The rattling of the chain through the hawse, decides it. A small settlement over which England's flag keeps guard, lies before us. This is the town of Victoria. This small island, previous to 1846, belonged to Borneo, but in that year the Sultan ceded it to Britain, as a convenient station for checking piracy on his sea-board. It lies off the north-eastern end of the great island of Borneo, and within view of its precipitous heights and mist-clad peaks.

December 14th.—Coaling is a long process at Lebaun, first, because the ship lies so far from the shore, and next, because of the insufficiency of convenient boats, and the necessary coolie labour to put the coal on board, thus it took us two whole days to get in as many hundred tons. By the evening of the 14th however, we had cleared the islands, and shaped course for Manilla against a head wind.

December 19th.—It has taken us twelve hours to clear the intricate, and gusty approaches to Manilla Bay, the wind, occasionally meeting us with such force, accompanied by such a chopping sea, that we sometimes made no progress at all. On coming to anchor we were rather surprised to find the " Lapwing " had preceded us, and was lying close in shore.

Manilla, the capital of Luzon, the largest of the Philippine Islands, is a city of considerable magnitude, and has all the appearance of a Spanish town in Europe, these islands having belonged to Spain for over 300 years.

Though we arrived on a Sunday it was anticipated there would be no difficulty in procuring coal immediately. Had the British been in authority here we should have been *privileged* to do so with impunity. When this conclusion was arrived at, one potent factor had not been considered—" the Church "—and for once in a way we were thankful to the Church. The archbishop of Manilla and his subordinates hold more real sway over the minds and bodies of the natives—Indians, as they are called—than all the temporal power of the governor, backed by his guards, or even than the king himself.

Amidst all the Spanish jabber around, it is refreshing to hear ourselves hailed in genuine English, and soon the author of the sound grasps us by the hand and welcomes us to his house, a request we gladly comply with.

The houses are very like those of Gibraltar, and one's memory is rapidly borne back to the "Rock," especially as everything around is Spanish.

Perhaps the great feature of the place is its cathedrals; one in particular, a magnificent structure, so roomy and lofty that I should think half the devout of the city could find accommodation therein. In less than two years subsequent to our visit the whole of this grand pile was little better than a heap of ruins, from an earthquake wave which passed over these islands. This most terrible of natural phenomena is of frequent occurrence in this quarter of the world. In many parts of the city we observed whole streets and churches in ruins, as if from a recent bombardment.

Cock-fighting is the great national sport, amusement, or cruelty, which of the three you will, indulged in by the good people of Manilla. Everywhere along the streets you may meet Spanish boys and half castes, with each his bird tucked under his arm ready for the combat, should the chance passer-by make it worth their while.

The best place to witness this propensity for blood, which seems in-born in every Spaniard, is at the public arena in the heart of the city, where hundreds of cocks are generally engaged at once, the betting on a certain bird not unfrequently amounting to thousands of dollars. I will not trouble you with the sickening details of the scene I witnessed—to my shame I say it—I think few of those who are present at a first exhibition of this cruel and useless sport will be desirous of witnessing a second—except he be a man of a morbid inclination. One may be impelled by curiosity to satisfy a human weakness, but every rightly balanced mind will turn from the scene with feelings of repugnance and disgust.

December 23rd.—The last day of our stay, and the last opportunity we shall have for laying in stock for the 25th. In the afternoon the caterers of messes having been accorded the necessary permission, went on shore to make a general clearance in the Manilla markets. There was every prospect, when they left the ship, of the day continuing fine—a bright sun and a clear sky above, and a smooth sea below. Unfortunately for the success of the expedition, this happy meteoric combination did not continue. The heavens began to frown, and the sea—ever jealous of its sister's moods—put on a restless appearance. At sun-down the wind suddenly rose to half a gale, with a cross lumpy sea and drenching showers of rain. The accommodation for the men to return to the ship was degrees from being called even fair. They had hired a rickety steam launch, scarcely capable of holding her own in ordinary weather, and two smaller boats, or gigs, neither of which was in a seaworthy condition; and in these was to be found room for upwards of forty men, besides about a ton of provisions of all kinds. It was evident, or ought to have been, that it was madness to attempt leaving the shore whilst the present weather lasted. I have seen the offence of breaking leave justified for less boisterous weather. Orders, however, (especially sailing orders) are imperative; so the flotilla put off at 7 p.m. in tow of the launch. The following was the arrangement:—The launch, laden far below her bearings, took the lead; the second boat contained all the heaviest provisions—flour, pigs, poultry, potatoes, and such like; whilst far too many men had stowed themselves in the third boat, to give but the faintest idea of either comfort or safety.

When about half-way to the ship, the painter of the hindmost boat parted, and the launch, rounding to, to her assistance narrowly escaped swamping. The next mishap chanced to the second boat—the provision gig—whose stem piece was tugged completely out of her, and the two sides, having thus lost their mutual support, parted and went to the bottom, the onlookers having to endure the melancholy sight of witnessing all their good things going to fatten old Davy Jones, or to fill his lockers, or something of that sort. But the distress of these very distressed mariners was not yet complete; a strange fatality seemed to have embarked with them. It was now the launch's turn: first the third boat, next the second, and now the launch in proper, though fortunately not arithmetical progression. It was discovered that the supply of coal could not possibly last to the ship! What was to be done? "Opportunity," it is said, "makes the thief;" it may be also said, with equal truth, that opportunity makes the dormant abilities of some men to soar above their fellows, over-riding even destiny itself. The Spanish crew of the launch were unequal to the emergency, were worse than useless in fact; but an able substitute for the engineer was found in Andrews, one of our leading stokers; and for coxswain, who better than Law, the boatswain's mate? The former of these at once directed everybody to pull the inner wood work of the launch to pieces, and, as the bump of destructiveness has its full development in the sailor phrenology, he had not long to wait for his fuel; thus they managed to reach the ship full six hours after they had left the shore.

December 25th.—Christmas in merry England is one thing; Christmas in a gale in the China Sea another, and so distinct a thing as scarcely to be confounded with the former. But let us see if we can tell our friends something about it. Considering the shortcomings we had to put up with—bare tables, hungry bellies, and the lively movements of our ship, consequent on a rising malevolent sea—I think we managed to enjoy a fair amount of fun, whether it was genuine or not is another point, nor would I like to vouch for its being altogether devoid of irony. "Father Christmas" paid us his customary visit anyway, in his mantle of snow—fancy snow within fifteen degrees of the line!—which merry, rubicund, and very ancient man was ably personated by a gigantic marine, the necessary barrel-like proportions being conveyed by a feather pillow.

"A hungry man is an angry one;" so runs the legend, but, if true, and I have every reason to believe that it is, it held not on the lower deck of the "Iron Duke" this day, for *no* man was angry, and *every* man *was* hungry, not counting some who had their heads down the lee scuppers. Altogether the day passed very smoothly inboard, though outside a storm was hurrying on us with gigantic strides.

December 26th.—The overcast sky of last night was indeed a precursor of what was to follow. About midnight the wind freshened into a full gale, the first we have encountered since leaving England. It gave us a proper shaking down into our places. The sea became wild and mountainous, the wind shrieking and vicious, and as to hold our course we had to stem its full fury, it was found impossible to keep the ship head on except at a much greater consumption of coal than we were prepared to use. Crash! What's gone? The jib-boom and all its appurtenances. The wrecked spar falling athwart the ram remained there for hours, proving a most difficult obstacle to clear away in such a whirl as was going on in the neighbourhood of our bows.

But there were no signs of the gale moderating, and the admiral deeming, I suppose, the present state of things far from satisfactory determined on putting back to Manilla. The ship was brought around, or "wore" as nautical men term it, an evolution which, though not of difficult accomplishment, at a certain moment in its progress leaves the vessel completely helpless in the trough of the sea, a fact you all know far better than myself, I only touch upon it to hint what the result must be to such a cumbersome mass as our iron hull. As we broached to, it became a matter of holding on to everything, and by everything—eyebrows and all—especially between decks. Delightful times these for ditty boxes, crockery, bread barges, and slush tubs; 'tis their only chance for enjoyment and they make the most of it. Such revelry generally winds up with a grand crash somewhere in the vicinity of the iron combings to the hatchways. Any plates left, any basins? Nay, that would be to ask too much of the potter's art. At length we are put round, and running back to Manilla under all the canvas we dare shew.

December 31st.—Completed with coal and left on a

fresh attempt to reach Hong Kong, the black and lowering sky suggesting either the continuation of, or the sequel to, the late stormy weather. Being New Year's Eve the usual attempt at a tin-pot band was made to make the night hideous. Setting aside the annoyance of this species of rowdyism to the less exuberant spirits amongst us, the noise would be most unseemly with the commander-in-chief on board, and it says much for the would-be musicians that they saw it in this light.

We reached the northern point of Luzon without mishap, and stood away with a heavy cross-sea for Hong Kong, arriving on January 4th, 1879.

CHAPTER VII.

"Then Kublai Khan gave the word of command
And they all poured into the Central Land."

HONG KONG.—SOME CHINESE MANNERS AND CUSTOMS.

I SUPPOSE there are few amongst us, sailors though we are, who, as boys at school when reading of China, have never expressed a wish to see that land for themselves, to say nothing of making the acquaintance of its quaint old-world people in their very own homes. In my imagination I had covered its goodly soil with wondrous palaces, all sparkling with splendour and embellished with all that art could furnish or riches command. I had peopled its broad plains with bright beautiful forms in silken attire, amongst whom a love of the elegant and the beautiful pervaded all classes of the community, and who in long ages ago had attained to arts and learning which it has taken us centuries of careful study and elaborate research to acquire. Yea, it was always a wonderland to me, even down to the present year; such is the power which the associations formed by the child exercise over the mind of the man. Yet were we prepared to meet a people who should, in almost all things, differ from almost all other peoples. In the last particular we are not deceived; in all else, yes. But I wont anticipate.

In this little book I shall not be able to tell you a tithe of what may be told of this land did I feel competent to do so. Volumes have been written on the subject, and still the half has not been said. I purpose, therefore, henceforward to intersperse with the narrative of our own doings, just so much of the manners and customs of the Chinese and Japanese, as every sailor possessed of the ordinary powers of vision may see for himself.

January 4th.—The harbour of Hong Kong is reached from the sea by means of a rather long and tortuous passage, with bleak barren heights on either hand,—the channel being in some parts so narrow that there is scarce room for the ship to turn.

The island itself—rendered either "*red harbour*" or "*fragrant streams*," which you prefer, though neither seems applicable, certainly not the latter if by *fragrance* is meant what we mean by it—lies on the southern seaboard of China. It became British in 1842, on the conclusion of the first Chinese war. The city of Victoria is situated on its northern side, and stands on a beautiful land-locked harbour, formed by the island on the one hand and the peninsula of Rowloon (also British) on the other a sheet of water which always presents a gay and animated appearance, from the thousands of vessels and boats which cover its surface like a mosaic.

It is not without some difficulty that we push our way through the thronging craft, principally little boats termed "sampans," to our moorings abreast of the Dockyard. Curious craft withal, and serving a double purpose; for besides their legitimate one, whole families live and move, are born, and die in them; the necessary accommodation being furnished by an ingenious arrangement of hatches, floors, and partitions, and, as it seems highly fashionable that the Chinese mammas should be making constant additions to the population, the squalling of the young celestials betrays a healthiness of lung, and a knowledge of its capabilities, scarcely to be credited of such small humanity.

The earlier fate of these infantile members of the boat population is sad. They are exposed to a "rough-and-tumble" existence as soon as they are ushered into the world, especially should the poor innocent have the misfortune to be born a girl baby, for in that case she has simply to shift for herself, the inhuman parents considering themselves fortunate if they lose a girl or two overboard. The boys, or "bull" children, as they are termed, meet with rather more care relatively speaking. As, from the nature of their occupation, but little time can be devoted to nursing—the mother being compelled to constant labour at the oar—the child is slung on to her back, and, as she moves to and fro with the stroke of the oar, the babe's soft face bobs in unison against its mother's back, a fact which will perhaps explain how it is that the lower class Chinese wear their noses flattened out on their two cheeks rather than in the prominent position usually selected by that organ.

It is amazing how wonderfully quick the Chinese pick up a colloquial foreign tongue; the same tailor for instance experiencing no difficulty in making himself understood in English, French, Russian, or Spanish; English, though, is the language par excellence along all the China seaboard. So universal is it that a foreigner must needs know something of our tongue to make himself intelligible to the ordinary Chinaman; and, more remarkable still, there is such a vast difference between the spoken dialects of north and south China—nay, even between any two provinces in the " Flowery Land "—that I have known some of our native domestics from the Canton district, when talking with their countrymen of Chefoo, communicate their ideas and wants in English, because their own medium failed them; the difference between the native dialects being as broad as that between English and Dutch.

Though such a diversity exists *orally*, the *written* character is common, and expresses exactly the same idea all over the empire, and beyond it in Japan, Çirea, and the Loo Choo islands.

The Chinese are splendid workmen, providing you can furnish them with a model or copy, for there is very little genius, properly so-called, attached to John Chinaman.

Their imitative faculty and powers of memory are really wonderful; as an instance of the former perhaps the following may not be amiss :—

" In the earlier days of the first occupation, the English residents of Hong Kong were often placed in difficulties about their clothing, Chinamen not having attained to that perfection in the tailors' art which they now have acquired. On one occasion an old coat was supplied to a native tailor as a guide to the construction of a new one; it so happened the old garment had a carefully mended rent in its sleeve—a circumstance the man was prompt to notice—setting to at once, with infinite pains, to make a tear of a similar size and shape in the new coat, and to re-sew it with the exact number of stitches as in the original."

The old stories we have heard at home about a Chinaman's tail being designed that by it he may be hoisted to heaven, and that if he lose it he may never hope to reach that desirable altitude, have really no foundation in fact, nor is it a fact, as sailors are apt to believe, that it is nurtured for their special benefit as a convenient handle for playing off practical jokes on the luckless possessors; the truth being that the "queue," now so universally prized amongst them, is a symbol of conquest forced upon them by their hated Tartar-masters. Previous to the seventeenth century the inhabitants of the middle kingdom wore their hair much after the style of the people of Cirea, but after the Manchu conquest they were compelled to adopt the present mode.

The city of Victoria is very prettily situated on the slopes of an eminence which culminates in a peak at an altitude of 1300 feet, and from which a most charming and cheerful view of the sea on the one side, and the harbour and the yellow sand-stone hills of China on the other.

It is allowed to be the most cosmopolitan city in the world. Representatives of races far in excess of the Pentecostal catalogue, may be encountered in its streets in any hour's walk; men of all shades of colour and of every religious creed live here side by side in apparent perfect harmony. The Chinese who form the bulk of the population live entirely apart from the "*Ung-moh*" (red hair devils) as they flatteringly term us. English manners and customs do not [seem to have influenced the native mind in the smallest degree, in spite of our charities and schools—a fact we cannot wonder at, taking into account our *diabolical* origin.

The town—by which I mean the European part of it—possesses many public and private buildings of almost palatial grandeur. Of these, Government house, the City hall—including the museum and reading room, the cathedral and college, the various banks, and the residences of the great merchants may be cited as examples. There is also a fine botanical garden, not nearly so large as that at Singapore, but perhaps scarcely less beautiful, and an extensive recreation and drill ground, where one may see curious sights! pigtailed, loose-robed Chinamen wielding the cricket-bat, and dealing the ball some creditable raps too.

There is perhaps only one good street in the colony, Victoria street or Queen's road; this traverses the city from end to end, and constitutes the great business thoroughfare of the place. After about an hour's walk along it, for the first part under an arcade of trees, we find ourselves in the filthy, unsavoury Chinese quarter, as the nose is careful to remind you if there be any doubt about it. They are certainly a very dirty race, these Chinamen; the dirtiest on earth, I should be inclined to say, considering their boasted civilization and vaunted morals; and, though compelled by our sanitary laws to live somewhat more cleanly than their enthralled brethren on the continent, still they are dirty, and I'll hazard to say a sight of the Chinese of this town would soon dispel any illusions one might have nourished to the contrary. A subsequent visit to the native city of Shanghai shewed us to what disgusting depths humanity can descend in this particular.

This enterprising people possess some very fine shops, where you can purchase every known European commodity at cheaper rates than of the European firms. Every shop has a huge sign-board depending from the top of the house to the bottom, whereon is recorded in vermillion and gold characters, not so much the name as the virtues of the man within, sometimes, too, his genealogical tree is appended. Such expressions as "no cheating here" or "I cannot deceive," are common, but, in nearly every case, belie the character of the proprietor, who is a living libel on the word honesty. Honesty! old Shylock even would blush for them.

Here, where there is protection for life and property, a shopkeeper surprises you at the rich and grand display of his wares. In China proper, a dealer dare not show all he is worth for fear of the mandarins, who, should one chance to pass that way, would in all probability, cast his covetous eyes on the poor man's property, and demand whatever had taken his fancy. Nor may a poor man be in possession of an article inconsistent with his position in the social scale—he may not be the owner of a tiger's skin, for instance, as none but mandarins and people of similar position, are permitted such luxuries. This reminds one of the time, not so very remote, when similar restrictions were placed on dress in England.

This system of mulcting is known all over China as "*cum-shaw*," a system, too, which I would advise all sailors to adopt in their dealings with the slippery race if they would not be robbed. The vendor dare not say nay to a mandarin; and, though it is a point of etiquette on the part of the big man to offer payment, it is equally a point of etiquette for the tradesman to refuse: a fact, it is said, the mandarin always calculates on.

In addition to the orthodox shop, the streets are lined with itinerants, orange stalls, betel-nut tables, heaps of rags, and sundries, baskets of vegetables of very strange appearance and strong penetrating odours, half-cooked roots and leaves—for the people never eat a well-cooked root or vegetable; it is from these principally that the intolerable stench is proceeding.

What the Chinese eat is a mystery, and such queer compounds enter into their *menu* that I would give everybody who dines with a Chinaman this advice—don't enquire too minutely into what is placed before you, or you will eat nothing, and so offend your host; bolt it and fancy it is something nice—and *fancy* goes for something at times, I can assure you. That it requires a tremendous effort on the part of the human stomach, the subjoined "Bill of Fare" of a dinner given to Governor Hennessey by one of the Chinese guilds will, perhaps, serve to shew:

---

* The *Holothuria* of naturalists—a species of sea-slug or sea-cucumber found on the shores of Borneo and on most of the islands of the Pacific, and which being dried in the sun is considered a dainty by Chinese epicures.

Birds' Nest Soup.
Pigeons' Egg Soup.
Fungus Soup.

Fried Sharks' Fins.
Beche-de-mer* and Wild Duck.
Stewed Chicken and Sharks' Fins.
Fish Maw.

Minced Partridge.
Ham and Capon.
Meat Ball and Fungus.
Boiled Shell Fish.
Pig's Throat, stewed.
Minced Shell Fish with Greens.
Chicken Gruel Salad.
Stewed Mushrooms.
Pig's Leg, stewed.

Roast Capon.	Roast Mutton.
Roast Pig.	Roast Goose.

Fruits.	Melon Seeds.
Preserves.	Almonds.

Cats, too, are entertained as food, though I believe only by the extremely poor, to whom nothing seems to come amiss. One may frequently meet in the streets vendors of poor puss, easily recognisable by their suggestive cry, "mow (miow?) youk"—cat-meat!

One is struck with astonishment at the vast crowds which always throng the streets, each unit of which seems intent on some most important business, and looks as though its accomplishment absorbed his whole being. Perhaps it is only a few ounces of fish which he carries suspended from his finger by a cord; but if it were the emperor's diamonds he could not conduct himself with more importance.

The ordinary means of conveyance in China is by the sedan chair, a sort of box of cane-work supported on poles for the convenience of the bearers, of whom there are generally two, but frequently as many as six. The riding is comfortable enough, and the springy motion imparted by the rider's weight is one of the pleasantest sensations I know of. Of course our tars, immediately they come on shore and see something new, want to find out all about it: hence sedan chairs are all the go, and a bad time the poor coolies have of it, too; for "Jack" is all motion, especially if he be in that semi-apathetic state known as "east half south," as it not unfrequently happens that he is. He compels his bearers to tax their powers of endurance to the utmost, urging them by all the endearing epithets in the nautical vocabulary to unheard-of exertions, regardless of the luckless pedestrians in the way.

Whilst we are on the return voyage through Queen's road, I must just say a word or two about the people's costume, which, as we observe, is nearly the same for both sexes; for if there be any difference, it is but slight in detail. Their dress is the most unbecoming and ungraceful it is possible to conceive, and yet, we are bound to admit, most refined. Had the women the redeeming quality of beauty, or the charm of a pretty face, possibly even this dress might appear to better advantage. A coarse-looking black or blue blouse, of that material known to us as "nankeen," a tiny apron confined to the waist by a slender scarlet cord—their only bit of bright color—short wide trousers, almost as broad at the bottoms as they are long, bare legs and feet—such is a vision of the Chinese woman of the working classes. The dress of a lady differs from this only in the nature of the material of which the garments are made—in their case, silk as a rule—stockinged feet, and silk shoes with thick white, though extremely light, soles. Nations, like individuals, have their fopperies; the celestials display this quality, particularly in the coverings for the feet. The shoe, especially of the females, is, beyond question, the most tasteful article in their costume. It is, as I have said before, made of silk, generally of a lavender, salmon, or rose color, embroidered in beautiful and artistic patterns of leaves, flowers, and insects. The soles are of the whitest doeskin; and so particular are they that they shall retain their unsullied appearance, that, like the cats, they seldom walk through a wet or muddy street.

The system of binding the feet of the women is by no means so universal as we have been led to believe, and we must confess to having been deceived in this matter; we all thought, probably, to have seen *all* the women with that useful member reduced to the dimensions of a baby's foot—instead of which, what do we really see? scarce one deformed woman in all our walks. Yet this nation considers this cramped, tortured lump (it has lost all semblance to a foot) an index of beauty.

Their hair is by far their finest possession, which, with their large almond-shaped eyes, is invariably of a black color. I once saw a Chinaman with *red* hair, and you cannot think how ludicrous his queue looked beside the sable tails of his brethren. The manner in which the women dress their hair is most wonderful, and materially helps to give them their uninviting appearance. They have a fashion of sticking it out around the head in the shape of a teapot, stiffened with grease and slips of bamboo. That this style of head-dress enhances their ugliness very few Europeans I think will deny; for some women whom we have seen, with their hair combed neatly back over their heads and coiled up in a trace behind, looked not altogether uncomely.

The head is dressed but once in ten days; and as the people sleep in their day clothes, the possibility is they entertain about their persons a private menagerie of those interesting creatures whose name looks so vulgar in print. It is one of the commonest scenes in the streets to see a Chinaman squat on the kerb-stone and turn up a fold or two of his trousers to manipulate these little pests; and even the high officials and well-to-do people look upon it as no outrage to the proprieties, to be seen removing one of "*China's millions*" from the garment of a friend or guest.

CHAPTER VIII.

———— " All the deep
Is restless change."   *   *   *

PREPARATIONS FOR THE NORTH.—AMOY.—WUSUNG, AND WHAT BEFELL US THERE.

WHATEVER pretensions to beauty our ship may have possessed on leaving England—and that she possessed some it is but fair to add—have been greatly marred by the late voyage, and especially by the washing down we encountered on the trip from Manilla. The effect has been to reduce our once fairy and glistening hull to a jaundiced mass of rust and stains. Therefore are we to go into "weeds." Black certainly gives an iron-clad a more man-of-war look, and a more war-like effect, to say nothing of the superior ease with which it can be kept clean.

January 22nd.—The Chinese new-year's day.—I should consider even such a poor account of the Chinese as this professes to be very incomplete, did it not contain something as to the manner the people observe the festival of the new year. And just a word before I start. It must not be supposed that I gained the information, if it be worthy to be classed as such, on a first visit to Hong Kong. This part of my "journal," including the previous chapter, has received the corrections and additions of nearly four years' experience.

The Chinese new year—a movable feast—depending, like all their chronological measurements, on the motions of the moon, may occur as early as it does this year, or it may fall as late as the middle of February. It is to the celestials what Christmas day is to us, and is observed by every true Chinaman most religiously: not, be it understood, religiously in our and the common acceptation of the term—for China has no religion—it possesses a gigantic superstition; but between a superstition and a religion, I need scarcely add, a vast difference exists. To the practical mind of John Chinaman, religious observances are made to subordinate themselves to worldly interests.

During the time we have been on the station the Shanghai district was once suffering from extreme drought. The rain-god was appealed to—still no rain came. Well, what was to be done? This. The god was admonished, that if rain came not within a certain period something terrible would happen to him. Still no rain. The exasperated priests and people then took measures to execute their threat. Putting a rope around the idol, the people, with their united efforts, pulled him to the ground to suffer further outrages at the hands of an ungrateful mob. Thus much for their *religion*. But to continue.

The last month in the old year is spent in elaborate preparation for the coming one. All arrears of business are made up, all accounts closed and punctually discharged, whilst everyone works his hardest to increase his stock of money.

At midnight on the last of the old year a bell is heard to toll, at which signal everybody rushes into the streets, armed with squibs, crackers, Catherine wheels, and other blatent pyrotechnical compositions; and as each tries to outdo his neighbour in the din he creates, the noise accompanying their discharge is the most satisfactory possible. The temples and pagodas are brilliantly lighted with colored lamps and colored candles, whilst similar candles and "joss-sticks," and gold and silver paper, illumine the interiors of their, at other times, grimy and dingy abodes. When morning arrives, the streets present a curious spectacle—everybody seems to be shaking hands with *himself*. A Chinaman, on meeting and saluting a friend, instead of seizing his hand, as we should, clasps his own hands together, the right hand grasping the left, which he sways up and down in front of his body.

Each person, too, is dressed in the newest and costliest dress he can afford; and as there is but one univeral fashion of garment in China, everybody tries to surpass everybody else in the richness of the material of which his clothes are made. The children, in particular, come out well, the girls especially, with highly-rouged and powdered cheeks and necks, gaudily decorated "queue" (for that appendix is not confined to the one sex), and silk dresses of the most beautiful colors. The whole scene has a very stage-like and brilliant effect.

It is worthy of remark, as shewing another trait in this truly remarkable race, that though they manufacture a very fiery liquor (called "*samshaw*") from rice, yet you will rarely see a drunken Chinaman in the streets. As far as I can remember I have met with only one such, and he a servant on board our ship, who had adopted a liking for rum because, I suppose, it is the custom for a sailor to drink what is issued to him.

The harbour, too, has its distinctive features on this gay and festive occasion. Every junk is covered with great pennons of silk in the most startling colors, whilst from every available space small oblong pieces of paper, with characters written on them, flutter to the breeze. These are "*joss-papers*," and contain prayers for wealth, prosperity, and (if they have not one already) an heir. "*joss*" is the generic name they give to their idols, and the whole ritual they call "*joss pidgin.*" The priests they name "*joss-men*," an appellation, too, they somewhat irreverently bestow on our naval chaplains. One of the largest junks, with a priest on board, and containing all the vessels and objects pertaining to their ritual, makes the circuit of the harbour—the priest meanwhile burning prayers and setting off crackers for a blessing on the supply of fish for the ensuing year.

January 29th.—This evening the officers gave their first theatrical entertainment on board, the acting of some of the characters being pronounced above the average; one or two of the younger midshipmen, to whom the parts fell, made very tempting and graceful ladies.

February 14th.—This day finds us at the back of the island preparing for target practice. In one of the bays here is an admirable natural target: a solitary rock rising perpendicularly from the sea, with a mark painted on it, is a most interesting thing to fire at, for you can observe the effect of your shot. Behind this rock sloped a hill, on which were seated, though unknown to us, two Chinamen; the first half-a-dozen rounds were so true that the unseen watchers had no suspicion they were in dangerous quarters, or that it was possible that even the Duke's marksmen were fallible; the seventh round disillusioned them, for, from a slight fault in the elevation, the shot over-reached the target and pitched so close to the Chinamen that stones and rubbish came rattling down from everywhere about their ears; fear lent them wings, and they scampered off like the wind. They may be running now for aught I know, as when we last saw them the horizon seemed to be the goal they were aiming at.

March 10th.—We were to have put to sea to-day had not a melancholy and fatal accident changed the whole course of events. Richard Darcy, a young seaman, whilst engaged on the crosstrees fell to the deck, striking the rail on the topgallant forecastle in his fall. His body was frightfully mangled and torn, his scull fractured, and all his limbs broken. Mercifully he never regained consciousness. Next day we buried him in the beautiful cemetery of Happy Valley, than which there are few more picturesque spots in China; 'twas surely a poetic fancy which inspired the Chinese with the term "*happy*" when naming this sylvian vale.

In the afternoon we slipped from the buoy and steamed seaward for tactics, returning the following day to prepare for going in dock.

March 26th.—The last day for our stay in Aberdeen. A special steam launch had arrived from Hong Kong during the forenoon with all the élite of the city to see the floating of our ship. However, they were doomed to disappointment, for, on the tide reaching its highest, it was found the ship refused to move, nor would she start, though every effort was made to coax her. It was not until the next tide, assisted by a strong breeze, that the ship once more rested in deep water.

With characteristic expedition and commendable zeal, our captain had the ship ready for sea, and awaiting orders in the briefest possible time.

April 21st.—Early this morning that pleasant sound, the cable rattling through the hawse, told us that we had bid good-bye to Victoria, for a few months at least. A rather stiff breeze was blowing at the time—a sufficient hint that we might possibly meet with something rash outside; nor was the hint to be disregarded, for, scarcely had we cleared the mouth of the harbour, when, what sailors call a "*sneezer*," accompanied by a green sea in all our weather ports, met us as an introduction to our northern cruise. So threatening was the look of the sky, and remembering that in these seas old Boreas often indulges his fancy in a gentle zephyr called a typhoon, it was deemed expedient to seek shelter for the night.

On the third day out we reached Amoy, or rather the outside anchorage of that harbour, to await daylight for the passage up to the town.

So far as the little island settlement forming the foreign concession can make it so, Amoy is a pretty enough place; otherwise it is like all other Chinese towns, and wont bear too close a scrutiny. It is built on an island of the same name, and is walled in by several miles of embrasured masonry; a fort or barracks on the beach, gay with pennons, imparting a semi-military look to the place. Flags seem to play a most important part in the usages of war amongst this nation, for, in addition to the great banners of the mandarins and their subordinates, every soldier bears one in the muzzle of his rifle, or stuck in a bamboo over his shoulder.

Resuming our course, after a stay of about forty-eight hours, we next touched at the island of White Dogs, off the port of Foo-Choo, the great naval depôt and arsenal of China. The "Vigilant" had preceded us here to embark the admiral for Foo-Choo, whilst we put to sea again.

April 30th.—At daylight we found ourselves amongst an archipelago of picturesque and richly cultivated islands, one mass of greenery from base to summit. The effect produced by the different tints of the foliage was very fine indeed. Beyond a doubt the Chinese exhibit great skill and economy in the gardener's art.

This was the approach to Chusan, the largest island of the group, at which we anchored at noon. The place fell under a British attack in 1841, remaining in our possession until the more convenient and more valuable island of Hong Kong was ceded to us in exchange. Before us lies a considerable town called Tinghae, where are buried many of our poor fellow countrymen and their families who fell victims to fever and the attacks of a cruel enemy during the occupation. We found their graves in a very neglected condition, many of the tombstones having been appropriated by the inhabitants to prop up those architectural abominations which it would be a libel to term houses. Admiral Coote subsequently sent the "Modeste" down with orders to repair the burial ground; the misappropriated stones were speedily restored to their places by the blue-jackets, who dealt with the natives in a very summary manner by wrecking their houses about their ears.

It was not long before a sleek old Chinaman, rejoicing in the imposing Chin-English name of "*Chin-Chang-Jim-Crow*," came on board and introduced himself as "me de bumboat"; he further explained that it was so long since a man-of-war had been in that neighbourhood, that probably he would experience some difficulty in procuring "*Chow*."

In the course of a day or so the admiral arrived from Ningpo, which was the signal for our at once heaving up anchor and continuing our voyage.

We are now in the estuary of one of the noblest rivers of the world, and the largest in China. It is estimated that this river, the Yang-tsze-Kiang, "Son of the Ocean," brings seaward, annually, as much solid matter as would make an island as large as Ireland! The navigation of its mouth is extremely dangerous, on account of the constantly-shifting sandbanks and consequent alteration of the channel. Fortunately, the European pilots are very skilful in detecting these changes. It is usual for large ships to drop anchor on this mud, locally termed the "flats," until boarded by a pilot, who takes you either to Wosung or Shanghai, according to your draught of water.

Wosung scarcely merits the name of town; perhaps

with more accuracy it might be termed a village. It is nevertheless, the head quarters of a large junk fleet, and has one of the finest and strongest forts in China to protect it from seaward. The place is interesting to us in one sense, because in 1875 an English company obtained permission to construct a line of rail from here to Shanghai.

China, with its four thousand years of existence, looked on this innovation with a jealous eye, and would have pitched the whole concern into the river, had she dared; unfortunately the line was carried near a burying ground, and thus a ready excuse for stopping the work presented itself. It was alleged that the noise would disturb the spirits of the dead, of whom the Chinese are in ghostly fear. An almost similar difficulty was met when the arsenal was built as Foo-Choo, and a magnificent temple was actually erected in that city for the accommodation of the refugee spirits.

To bring matters to a climax a man was run over by one of the trucks and killed. The mandarins could no longer hold out against the popular voice, and the whole plant was bought up by the Government for twice the sum the projectors had spent about it.

This is the brief history of the first and, up to now, the only attempt to introduce railways into China; but the late Kuldja difficulty, and the ease with which the Russians had brought an army to their Siberian frontier, have caused the Chinese to open their eyes to the advantage of railways for strategic, if for no other purpose, and I believe a line is already in contemplation between Tien-tsin and the capital.

Owing to a blunder on the part of the pilot, so some

said, and some others, in consequence of someone else's blunder, our anchor was dropped too near a mud bank, with the result that when the ship swung to a firm knot current, up she went high and dry. Means were at once taken to get her off, but by the time all the necessary arrangements were completed—and there was no time lost either—the tide had ebbed considerably.

In the middle watch of this, the "Iron Duke's" first night on the Chinese territory, the steel hawser was brought to the capstan, but a piece of yarn would have been equally efficacious; for, under the immense strain, it snapped like a bow string, and, as there was now nothing to keep the stern in check, away she went broadside on to the difficulty.

Meantime a telegram had been wired to the admiral at Shanghai, and next day all the available help at that port came down the river to our assistance; besides the "Vigilant," "Eyera," "Midge," and "Growler," there were two American war vessels, the "Monocasy" and "Palos," also a Chinese paddle steamer.

On the third night a combined attempt was made to either haul us off or to pull us to pieces. With all their tugging they effected neither the one nor the other, and, had not nature "lent us a fin"—in the shape of a breeze of wind—we might have been lying there to this day; a few pulls on our hawsers and we had the satisfaction of feeling that the dear old craft was once more on her proper element. The commander of one of the American ships afterwards commenting on the difficulty experienced in removing us, hailed our captain with "Guess, Cap'n, that piece of machinery of yours is lumpy!" "Rather, Jonothan, I calculate."

Had we not floated to-day the alternative was rather consoling; nothing less than the removal of all our heavy guns and spars.

Before our departure Shanghai was all astir at the visit of General Grant of the United States. Ostensibly, the general is travelling *incog.*, but really as the representative of the United States, for he flies the "stars and stripes" at the main, and gets a salute of twenty-one guns wherever he goes. For some reason or other we did not salute as he passed up the river.

May 22nd saw us clearing out of the dangerous precincts of the Shanghai river and shaping our course across the turbid waters of the Yellow Sea for pastures new—that is to say—for Japan. Under double-reefed canvas and a nine knot breeze we sighted land in the vicinity of Nagasaki on the 25th, and by evening our anchor "kissed the mud" in as lovely a spot as ever mortal set eyes on. But I will reserve my eulogies for another chapter.

CHAPTER IX.

> "It was a fresh and glorious world,
> A banner bright that shone unfurled
> Before me suddenly."

ARRIVAL AT NAGASAKI.—SOMETHING ABOUT JAPAN.—A RUN THROUGH THE TOWN.—VISIT TO A SINTOR TEMPLE.

I KNOW not if the author of the above lines had ever been to Japan. I should think it very unlikely; and possibly the poet is but describing the scenery of his Cumberland home. In no disparagement of the beauteous country of the lake and mountain, yet we must confess that nothing there can compare with Japan's natural magnificence.

All who have ever written of Japan, or who have ever visited its shores, are unanimous in the praise they bestow on its charms of landscape. Even rollicking and light-hearted tars, who, as a rule, are not very sensible to the beauties of nature, are bound to use "unqualified expressions of delight, when that "bright banner" lies unfurled under their gaze. And of all this beauteous land no part of it is more beautiful than the bay of Ommura, in the month of May.

Coming towards Nagasaki, from the westward, is like sailing on to a line of high, rigid, impenetrable rocks, for, apparently, we are heading blindly on to land which discloses not the slightest indication of an opening; but, relying on the accuracy of our charts, and the skill of our officers, we assume we are on the right course. By-and-bye the land, as if by some magic power, seems to rend asunder, and we find ourselves in a narrow channel, with well-wooded eminences on either hand, clothed with handsome fir trees. Right in front of us, and hiding the view of the town, is a small cone-shaped island of great beauty. English is a weak language in which to express clearly its surpassing loveliness. This is Takabuko, or more familiarly, Papenberg, a spot with a sad and bloody history, for it was here that the remnant of the persecuted Christians, who escaped the general massacre in 1838,—when 30,000 perished—made a last ineffectual stand for their lives and faith. But to no purpose, for pressed to extremities by the swords of their relentless persecutors, they threw themselves over the heights, and perished in the sea.

The people are not altogether to blame for this barbarous and cruel persecution. Had the Jesuits been satisfied with their spiritual conquests, and not sought to subvert the government of the country, all might have gone well, and Japan, ere now, been a Christian country. But no; true to themselves and to their Order, they came not to bring peace, but literally a sword, and the innocent were made to suffer for the ambitions of a few designing priests.

The island passed, what a view presents itself! The long perspective of the bay, the densely wooded hills and lower slopes, teeming with agricultural produce, rich corn fields, ripe for the sickle; picturesque dwellings, hid in shadowy foliage, and flowers and fruit trees, to which the purity and rarity of the atmosphere lend a brilliancy of colouring and distinctness of outline, impossible to describe; the clear blue water, with here and there a quaint and curious-looking junk, resting on its glassy and reflecting surface; the town, sweeping around the shores of the bay; and, afar, the majesty of hill and vale; such, dear reader, is a weak and very imperfect word picture of the charming bay of Omura.

Recent events in Japan have taken such a remarkable turn, that history, neither ancient nor modern, presents no parallel with it. That we may have a more adequate conception of the Japan of to-day, it is absolutely necessary that we make some acquaintance with the Japan of the past.

Of the origin of the people we can gleam very little, except from the questionable source of tradition. Several theories are advanced to account for their existence here. One authority discovers in them the long-lost "lost tribes of Israel;" according to another, they are a branch of the great American-Indian family; both of which statements we had better accept with caution. Their own theory—or rather that of the aborigines, the Aïnos of Yeso,—a race whom the indefatigable Miss Bird has recently brought prominently before the world—states that the goddess of the celestial universe, a woman of incomparable beauty and great accomplishments, came eastward to seek out the most beautiful spot for a terrestrial residence, and at length chose Japan, where she spent her time in cultivating the silkworm, and in the Diana-like pursuits of the chase; until one day, as she stood beside a beautiful stream, admiring her fair form in its reflecting surface, she was startled by the sudden appearance of a large dog. Tremblingly she hid herself, but the dog sought her out, and, to her surprise, entered into conversation with her, and finally into a more intimate alliance. From the union of these two opposite natures—according to this account—the Aïnos are descended.

One other tradition I will mention—the Chinese—which perhaps has something of the truth in it. According to it, a certain emperor of China, ruminating on the brevity of human life, and of his own in particular, thought it possible to find a means whereby his pleasant existence might be indefinitely prolonged. To this end he summoned all the physicians in his kingdom, and ordered them, on pain of forfeiting their heads, to discover this remedy. After much deliberation, one at last hit upon a plan which, if successful, would be the means of saving, at least, his own head. He informed the emperor that in a land to the eastward, across the Yellow Sea, was the panace he sought; but that, in order to obtain it, it was necessary to fit out a ship, with a certain number of young virgins, and an equal number of young men of pure lives, as a propitiatory offering to the stern guardian of the "elixir of life." The ship sailed, freighted as desired, and after a few days reached the western shores of Japan, from whence, you will readily imagine, the wily sage never returned. These young men and maidens became the ancestors of the Japanese race.

G

Their form of government was despotic in its character, and feudal in its system. The country was governed by a powerful ruler with the title of mikado—" son of the sun "—who was supported in his despotism by tributary princes, or daimios. Of them the mikado demanded military service in time of war, and also compelled them to reside a part of each year in his capital, where quarters were provided for them and their numerous retainers in the neighbourhood of the palace. The visitor may still see whole streets in Tokio without a single inhabitant, the former residences of the daimios' followers, and the aspect is dreary in the extreme.

In addition to his temporal functions, the mikado has always been the great high priest of the Sintor faith. On the breaking out of a war with China, it was found that his attendance with the army would deprive the religion of its spiritual head, and so indispensable was his presence in the great temple, that such a deprivation would be little short of a calamity. In this dilemma, he called to his aid the general of his forces, an able warrior and a shrewd designing man, conferred on him the hereditary title of shio-goon, or tycoon, and despatched him at the head of the army to carry fire and sword into the coasts of China. This prince's name was Tycosama, a name great in Japan's history, and destined to become terrible to the Christians. As generally happens, when a clever soldier with a devoted army at his back is placed in such a position, he finds it but a step to supreme dominion, the army being a pretty conclusive argument in his favor. His first act was the removal of the mikado to the holy city, Kivto, where henceforth he was kept secluded, and hemmed in by so much mystery, that the people began to look upon their ancient ruler as little less than a god.

It will be readily imagined that the tycoons, by their arrogant assumption to the imperial dignity, made for themselves many enemies amongst the powerful daimios. The disaffected united to form a party of reaction which, in the end, overthrew the tycoon, restored the mikado to his ancient splendour, and gave Japan to the world. In 1853, an American squadron, under Commodore Perry, came to Yokohama, and demanded a trade treaty with the United States. After much circumlocution he obtained one, thus pioneering a way for the Europeans. England demanded one the following year, and got it; then followed the other maritime nations of Europe, but these treaties proved to be of as little value as the paper on which they were drawn up.

The adherents of the tycoon displayed a bitter animosity against the foreigner, and especially a most powerful daimio, the prince of Satsuma, who nourished a detestable hatred to Europeans. Through the machinations of this party, murders of foreigners, resident in Yokohama, were of almost daily occurrence, till at last the British consul fell a victim to their hatred. This brought matters to a head. In 1863, England declared war against Japan; blockaded the Inland Seas with a combined squadron of English, French, Dutch, and American ships. acting under the orders of Admiral Keuper, stormed and captured Simonoseki, and burnt Kagosima, the capital of the prince of Satsuma. Having brought the Japanese to their senses, we demanded of them a war indemnity, half of which was to be paid by Satsuma.

Five years passed. The mikado meanwhile had placed himself at the head of the reactionary party, pensioned the tycoon, and made rapid advancement in European manners and customs. In 1868, Satsuma and his party broke out into open rebellion against the mikado. But the prince's levies were no match for the imperial troops, armed with the snider, and the result was the rebellion, after some sanguinary battles, was put down, the estates of the rebels confiscated, and the chief actors in the drama banished to distant parts of the empire.

There, dear reader, I am as glad as you that I have finished spinning that yarn. Now for the legitimate narrative.

Nagasaki, or more correctly Nangasaki, is a town of considerable magnitude, skirting the shores of the bay, and built in the form of an amphitheatre. On the terraces above the town, several large temples with graceful, fluted, tent-like roofs, embowered in sombre and tranquil pine groves, shew out distinctly against the dark background, whilst the thousands of little granite monumental columns of the burying grounds, stud the hills on every side, giving to Nagasaki almost a distinct feature.

Immediately ahead of the anchorage is the small island of Desima, the most interesting portion of the city to Europeans. Previous to 1859 it was the only part of Japan open to foreigners, and even then only to the Dutch, who, for upwards of 200 years, had never been allowed to set foot outside the limits of the island,—a space 600 feet long by 150 feet broad—separated from the main land by the narrowest of canals.

Japanese towns are laid out in regular streets, much after the fashion obtaining in Europe. The system of drainage is abominable, though personally, the people are the cleanest on earth, if constant bathing is to be taken as an index to cleanliness. The streets have no footpaths, and access to the houses is obtained by three or four loose planks stretching across the open festering gutters. As a natural result, small pox and cholera commit yearly ravages amongst the populace. Another great evil against good sanitation, exists in the shallowness of their graves. The Japanese have also a penchant for unripe fruits.

A native house is a perfect model of neatness and simplicity. A simple framework, of a rich dark coloured wood, is thrown up, and roofed over with rice straw. There is but one story, the requisite number of apartments being made by means of sliding wooden frames, covered with snow-white rice paper. The floor is raised off the ground about eighteen inches, and is covered with beautiful and delicately wrought straw mattresses, on which the inmates sit, recline, take their meals, and sleep at night. These habitations possess nothing in the shape of furniture; no fireplace even, because the Japanese—like Chinese—never use fire to warm themselves, the requisite degree of warmth being obtained by the addition of more and heavier garments. These abodes present a marked contrast to the Chinese dwellings, which, as we saw, were foul and grimy, whilst here all is cheerful and airy.

No house is complete without its tiny garden of dwarf trees, its model lakes, in which that curiosity of fish-culture, the many tailed gold and silver fish, are to be seen disporting themselves; its rockeries spanned by bridges; its boats and junks floating about on the surface of the lakes, in fact a Japanese landscape in miniature.

It seems the privilege of a people, who live in a land where nature surrounds them with bright and beautiful forms, to, in some manner, reflect these beauties in their lives. This people possess these qualities in an eminent degree, for a happier, healthier, more cheerful race, one will rarely see. Their children—ridiculously like their seniors from wearing the same style of garment—are the roundest, rosiest, chubbiest little pieces of humanity ever born. Everybody has a fresh, wholesome look, due to repeated ablutions. The bath amongst the Japanese, as amongst the ancient Romans, is a public institution; in fact, we think too public, for both sexes mix promiscuously together in the same bath, almost in the full light of day; whilst hired wipers go about their business in a most matter-of-fact manner. This is a feature of the people we cannot understand, but they themselves consider it no impropriety. A writer on Japan, speaking of this says :—"We cannot, with justice, tax with immodesty the individual who, in his own country, wounds none of the social proprieties in the midst of which he has been brought up." These bath-houses are perfectly open to the public gaze, no one evincing the slightest curiosity to look within, except, perhaps, the diffident sailor. It is very evident that Mrs. Grundy has not yet put in her censorious appearance in Japan, nor have our western conventionalities set their seal on what, after all, is but a single act of personal cleanliness. "*Honi soit qui mal y pense.*"

Their mode of dress is an embodiment of simplicity and elegance. Both sexes wear a sort of loose dressing gown, sometimes of silk—mostly so in the case of the fair sex—crossed over the front of their bodies, allowing the knee perfect liberty to protrude itself, if it is so minded, and confined to the waist by a band. But it is more particularly of the dress of the ladies I wish to speak. The band circling the waist, and known as the "*obe*," is very broad, and composed of magnificent folds of rich silk, and tied up in a large quaint bow behind. A Japanese lady lavishes all her taste on the selection of the material and in the choice of colour, of which these bands are composed, and which are to them what jewellery is to the more refined Europeans. No ornament of the precious metal is ever seen about their persons. Their taste in the matter of hues is faultless; no people, I will venture to say, have such a perception of the harmonies of colour. Their tints are of the most delicate and charming shades the artist's fancy or the dyer's art can furnish, and often wrought in rich and elegant patterns. They are passionately fond of flowers, the dark and abundant tresses of their hair being always decorated with them, either real or artificial. Their only other adornments are a tortoise-shell comb of delicate workmanship, and a long steel pin with a ball of red coral in the end, passing through their rich raven hair. They use powder about their necks and shoulders pretty freely, and sometimes colour the under lip a deep carmine, or even gold, (a process which does not add to their personal attractions. They wear no linen; a very thin chemise of silk crepe, in addition to the loose outer garment, is all their covering. But it must be remembered that the great aim of this people seems to be simplicity, therefore we wont too minutely scrutinize their deficiencies of costume; there is much to be said in its favour, it is neither immodest nor suggestive. The feet are clothed in a short sock, with a division at the great toe for the passage of the sandal strap. These sandals or clogs are the most ungainly articles in their wardrobe. A simple lump of wood, the length and breadth of the foot, about two or three inches in altitude, and lacquered at the sides, is their substitute for our boot. Their walk is a shuffling gait, the knee bent and always in advance of the body.

The married women have a curious custom—now fast dying out—of blacking their teeth and plucking out their eye-brows to prevent, as their husbands say, other men casting "sheep's eyes" at them.

The males of the coolie class are very scantily clad, for all that they wear is the narrowest possible fold of linen around the loins; but, as if to compensate for this scarcity of rigging, they are frequently most elaborately tattooed from head to foot.

A Japanese husband does not make a slave of his wife, as is too often the case amongst orientals; she is allowed perfect liberty of action, and to indulge her fancy in innocent pleasures to an unlimited extent. Her lord is not ashamed to be seen walking beside her, nor does he think it too much beneath him to fondle and carry the baby in public. They are excessively fond of their children; the hundreds of toy shops and confection stalls about the streets bearing testimony to this.

The old custom of dressing the hair, which some of

the men still affect, is rather peculiar. A broad gutter is shaved from the crown of the head forward, whilst the remaining hair, which is permitted to grow long, is gathered and combed upwards, where the ends are tied, marled down, and served over (as we should say in nautical phraseology) and brought forward over the shaven gangway.

One other custom I must mention, the strangest one of all: they have a legalized form of that vice which, in other countries, by tacit consent, is banned, but which even the most refined people must tolerate. But what makes it more strange still is, that no inconsiderable portion of the public revenue is derived from this source. The government sets aside a certain quarter in every city and town for its accommodation, gives it a distinct and characteristic name, and appoints officers over it for the collection of the revenues. I thought it not a little significant on landing for the first time in Japan to find myself and "rick-sha" wheeled, by the accommodating coolie, right into the heart of this quarter. The advances of the fair sex are likely to prove embarrassing to the stranger, for, before they are married, they are at liberty to do as they please, and do not, by such acts, lose caste or forfeit the respect of their friends and neighbours.

Here, as in the Indian Seas, our *laundresses* are men, the cleanest and quickest washers we have encountered in the voyage. As an instance of their despatch, they will take your bedding ashore in the morning, and by tea-time you will receive it ready for turning in, the blanket washed and dried, the hair teazed and made so soft that you would scarcely fancy it was the same old "doss" again.

Though the women do not wash our clothes, they do what is far harder work, *i.e.* coal our ship. We were surprised, beyond measure, to see women toiling away at this dirty, laborious calling. And the Japanese women are such little creatures, too! There was, however, one exception, a woman of herculean strength and limb, looking like a giantess amongst her puny sisters, and fully conscious of her superior muscular power. This lady, stripped to the waist as she was, would, I am sure, intimidate the boldest mariner from a too close acquaintance with her embrace. They belong to the coolie class, a distinct caste in Japan, wear a distinguishing badge on their clothing, form a community amongst themselves, and rarely marry out of their own calling.

At noon these grimy Hebes, Hercules as well, all tripped on board to dine, the upper battery offering them all the accommodation they required; each carried with her a little lacquered box, with three sliding drawers, in which was neatly and cleanly stowed her dinner—rice, fish, and vegetables; taking out all the drawers, and laying them on her lap, with a pair of chop-sticks, she soon demolished her frugal meal. After a whiff or two at a pipe, whose bowl just contained enough tobacco for two draws, she was ready to resume her work.

The European concession occupies the most picturesque position in Nagasaki, from which city it is separated by a creek, well known to our blue-jackets, spanned by two or three bridges. On either side of this strip of water a perfect cosmopolitan colony of beer-house keepers have assembled, with the sole intention of "bleeding" the sailor, and upon whose well-known devotion, to the shrine of Bass and Allsop, they manage to amass considerable fortunes.

Before leaving Nagasaki I would ask you to accompany me to one of the temples, that known as the Temple of the Horse, being, perhaps, the best. It is rather a long distance by foot, but Englishmen, at least according to Japanese ideas, have too much money to walk when they can ride, so to keep up the national conceit, but more for our own convenience, we jump into an elegant little carriage, or "*jin-riki-sha,*" literally "*man-power-carriage,*" but in sailor phrase "johnny-ring-shaw," or short "ring shaw." Away we go, a dozen or more in a line, over the creek bridge, past Desima, which we leave on our left hand, and soon we are in the heart of the native city, and traversing what is popularly known as "curio" street. At this point we request our human horses to trot, instead of going at the mad speed usual to them, in order that we make notes of Japanese life by the way. We pass many shops devoted to the sale of lacquer ware, for which the Japanese are so justly famed, catch glimpses of unequalled egg shell, and Satsuma china, made of a clay, formed only in this neighbourhood, and which, thanks to the European mania for collecting, fetch the most fancy prices; get a view of silk shops, full of rich stuffs and embroideries. Here an artist tinting a fan or a silk lantern; there a woman weaving cloth for the use of her household and everywhere people plying their various callings on the elevated floors of their houses. I should say needle making amongst these people is a rather laborious undertaking, and one which requires more than an ordinary amount of patience. The wire has first to be cut the desired length, then filed to a point at one end and the other flattened ready for the eye to be drilled, and finally the whole has to be filed up and smoothed off, and all by one man. The Japanese are but indifferent sewers, all their seams exhibiting numerous "holidays." Pretty children, with their hair clipped around their heads like a priest's tonsure, sport around us, but are not intrusive. Each child has a little pouch attached to his girdle, which, we are informed, contains the address of the child's parents, and also an invocation to the little one's protecting god, in case of his straying from home. We meet with cheerful looks and pleasant greetings everywhere. The gentle and musical "*o-hi-o*," "*good day*," with its softly accented second syllable, and as we pass the earnest "*sayonara*," the "*au revoir*" of the French, tell us very plainly we are no unwelcome visitors, whilst their bows are the most graceful, because natural, and therefore unaffected, actions it is possible to conceive.

We notice, too, that numbers of the males are in full European costume, which generally hangs about them in a most awkward manner, reminding one of a broom-handle dressed in a frock coat. Others, again, don't discard the national dress altogether, but compromise matters by putting on, in addition their long gown, a European hat and shoes, which, if anything, looks worse still. The ladies have not yet adopted the European style which, perhaps, they have sense enough to see, is far more complex and inconvenient than their own. Of this much I am certain that no mysterious production of Worth would be more becoming, or suit them better than their own graceful, national dress.

At our imperative "*chop, chop,*" jack's sole stock-in-trade of that intellectual puzzle, the Chinese language, and which he finds equally serviceable this side the water, our Jehus start off like an arrow shot from a bow. What endurance these men possess, and what limbs!

After a pleasant half-an-hour's ride, a sudden jolt indicates we are at our destination.

We alight at the base of a flight of broad stone stairs leading to the temple, and which we can just discern at a considerable altitude above us, peeping out of the dark shadow of a grove of firs. Arches of a curious and simple design, under which it is necessary to pass, are the distinguishing features of a kami or sintoo temple, and perhaps of Japan itself, as the pyramids are characteristic of ancient Egypt.

Two uprights of bronze, stone, or wood, inclined to each other at the summits, and held in position by a transverse beam piercing the pillars at about three feet from their tops. Over this again is another beam with horn-like curves at the ends, and turned upward, and simply laid on the tops of the shafts. The approaches to some of these temples are spanned by hundreds of such structures, which, when made of wood and lacquered bright vermillion, look altogether curious.

On the topmost stair, as if guarding the main entrance to the sanctuary, are two seated idols of the "god of war," in complete armour, each with bow in hand and a quiver full of arrows over his shoulder, and protected by a cage work of wire. What certainly gives us matter for speculation, and causes us no little surprise, is to see the golden scales of their splendid armour, and even their ruddy lacquered faces, bespattered with pellets of chewed paper after the manner familiar to us as school boys; when not satisfied with the correctness of the geographers, we used to chew blotting paper to fling in recent discoveries on the wall maps. Do these people desecrate their idols thus? There is no desecration here. These little lumps of pulp are simply *prayers*, pieces of paper on which the priests have traced some mystic characters for the use of the devout, and which, because of their inability to reach the idol to paste the strips on, they shoot through the wire in this manner.

We now pass under the last arch, with its monstrous swinging paper lantern, into the courtyard of the temple. The first object which claims our attention is a bronze horse, from which the temple takes its name. The work of art—for so it is reckoned—would be more like a horse, if its tail were less suggestive of a pump handle. Near is a bronze trough filled with holy water, to be applied internally; and around three sides of the square numerous empty houses, which, on high days and holidays, are used as shops for the sale of sacred and fancy articles. Up a few more steps and suddenly we are on the polished floor of the temple, and standing amidst a throng of kneeling worshippers, with heads bowed and hands pressed together in prayer.

Their mode of procedure at these shrines seems something after the following: the worshipper first seizes a straw rope depending from the edge of the roof of the temple, to which is attached a bell, of that shape worn by ferrets at home, only of coure on a much more gigantic scale; this is to apprise the slumbering god of the applicant's presence. He then commences his petition or confession; places an offering of money in a large trough-like receptacle for the purpose; takes a drink at the holy water font, and departs to his home chatting gaily to his neighbours as he descends the steps. The whole business occupies about five minutes.

Sintoo temples have but little interior or body. All the worshipping is done outside on the beautifully kept polished floor. A notice in English reminds us vandals that we must remove our shoes if we would tread this sacred spot.

Within, is simplicity itself; a mirror and a crystal ball is all one sees; the former typical of the ease with which the Almighty can read our hearts; the second an emblem of purity. They worship the Supreme Being under the threefold title, which, strangely enough, we find in the Book of Daniel, by which we may infer they have no inadequate conception of the true God.

We leave the temple court by a different outlet to that by which we entered, and come out on a charmingly laid out garden and fish ponds, where are seats and tea houses for the accommodation of visitors. Each tea house has its bevy of dark-eyed houris, who use every wile and charm known to the sex, to induce you to patronise their several houses. To do the proper thing, and perhaps influenced by the bright eyes raised so beseechingly to ours, we adjourn to one of these restaurants. Removing our shoes—a proceeding you are bound to comply with before entering a Japanese house—we seat ourselves cross-legged, tailor fashion, on the straw mattresses I have previously mentioned, whilst an attendant damsel, with deft fingers, makes the tea in a little terra-cotta teapot, the contents of which she poured into a number of doll's cups, without handles, on a lacquered tray. Other girls handed us each a cup, in which was a liquid not unlike saffron water in colour and in taste.

They use neither milk nor sugar, and the cups are so provokingly small, that it is only by keeping our attendant syrens under the most active employment, that we are at last able to say we have tasted it. With our tea we get some excellent sponge cake called "*casutira*," a corruption of the Spanish word "castile," said to be, until very recently, the only word of European etymology in the language. The Jesuits first introduced the cake from Spain, and taught the people how to make it. Whatever its origin, it is very good. You get chop-sticks handed you too, which, after a few ineffectual and laughable attempts to manipulate in the approved fashioh, you throw on one side. After the decks are cleared the young ladies bring out their *sam-sins*, and whilst we smoke Japanese pipes, they delight our ears with an overture, which we pronounce excruciating in English, though with our eyes we say "divine as Patti."

But we must not tarry longer here for the setting sun warns us it is time to get on board.

Our patient "steeds" are at the foot of the stairs, each ready to claim his rider. These fellows will stick to you like a leech; follow you about for hours, never intruding their presence on you, and yet seem to anticipate all your movements and wants.

CHAPTER X.

"I looked upon those hills and plains,
And seemed as if let loose from chains,
To live at liberty."

THE INLAND SEAS.—KOBE.—FUSI-YAMA.—YOKOHAMA. VISIT TO TOKIO.

THE arrival of the "Vigilant" from Shanghai, with the admiral on board, brought our stay at charming Nagasaki to a close. During the absence of our band with the "Vigilant," one of its members, Henry Harper, a feeble old man, and far advanced in consumption, died at Shanghai.

June 11th.—Left Nagasaki *en route* for the eastward, *via* the Inland Seas. Our way to Simoneski lay through numerous islands of so beautiful an appearance that a writer has compared them to some of the fairest spots in Devon. But this, though it says much, is but a poor tribute to such enchanting loveliness.

At daylight the following morning we made the narrow channel at Simoneski, the western entrance to the seas; and as there is always a strong rush of water through the passage towards the ocean, we had to steam hard against a considerable current. The town, of which I spoke in my last chapter, has a very straggling and neat cleanly appearance. There are no forts or other defences to indicate that not so long ago this town offered defiance and a short resistance to a European squadron.

The Inland Sea has four chief divisions, which now commences to open out before us, and is reckoned to possess some of the finest scenery in the world. I had often wished to see it for myself; but I must confess I was unprepared, even with an imagination not liable to surprise, at a picture of nature's own producing, for such beauty and grandeur. For hundreds of miles, day after day, we were borne past a moving diorama of scenery unrivalled by anything here below. On a smooth blue sea, and under a cloudless sky, onward we sped, passing, one after another, the most delightful islets the eye ever dwelt on, each appearing to us a perfect paradise in itself. Further on, indicated by a mere purple haze, appeared others, and yet others, in almost endless perspective. I should say the islands in this sea may 'be numbered by thousands.

Not many years since, strangers were debarred from using this passage. I fancy I can imagine the impressions the first Europeans must have had of this fairy land, of such a climate, such a soil, and such delightful glades and woodlands!

On each of the larger islands we noticed snug temples, like miniature Swiss châlets, embowered in woods—their peculiar architecture standing out in relief from a tangled mass of vegetation.

The channels where there are so many islands as here are necessarily intricate and dangerous; and as it would be to court danger to continue our course after sundown, there are several well-marked anchorages where it is customary to bring up at night. The first of these was a sheltered bay with twin villages at its head, which I fancifully designated Kingsand and Cawsand—the promontory forming one arm of the bay, looking not unlike Penlee point—greatly adding to the conceit.

June 14th.—At noon we reached Kobé, or Hiogo, and let go our anchor far out in what appears to be an open roadstead. This town is one of the most recent of the treaty ports—in fact it and Osaca opposite, are the last thrown open to trade; hence we shall probably find Kobé more *native* and less Europeanized than are the other towns we shall visit.

The native town is very extensive, reaching far back to the basis of the hills, and well away to the left of the anchorage. To the right a stretch of low-lying land, with its tiny fields of ripe grain, looks very fine. This track leads to the water-falls—a prettier place for a pic-nic and one more accommodating one can scarcely find. Between this plain and the old town of Hiogo the Europeans have raised their pretty picturesque dwellings. The streets here are very regular and well kept, the trees planted along the sides giving the place quite a French appearance.

There is at least one I was about to say magnificent street in the town, with an extent of over two miles, along and in which all the bustle and business are conducted. Notwithstanding its recent opening, public-houses, with their alluring signs, have sprung up with mushroom-like rapidity. One in particular I will just mention, not that you are ever likely to forget "Good old Joe," but simply that you may smile, when reading this over, at the willingness with which you were led as lambs to the slaughter. I trust you escaped without the mark of the butcher's knife.

After traversing about half the length of the street I mentioned before, the traveller finds himself abreast of the Nanko temple, a large and imposing structure having a wide and noble-looking entrance from the street, and just now presenting a very festive and animated appearance. On either side the really grand avenue to the temple a veritable fair is being held, and such a spectacle was as welcome as it was unlooked for. The amusements were so like those provided at similar gatherings at home that the wonder is, that peoples separated by half a world of varied civilization can possess the details of such festivities in common. Confection stalls, wild beast shows, shooting galleries, archery grounds, theatres, music halls, even a Japanese edition of the thimble-and-pea business was not wanting. In one of the theatres we visited, the acting, although considered good from a Japanese point of view, possessed too many muscular contortions, too much contraction and expansion of the facial organs, to please an English audience. Men do all the acting, women never appear on the Japanese stage.

The music halls are not more enlivening than are the theatres, though the sight of an interior is worth the ten *sen* fee, if only to see their manner of conducting the opera. If you imagine the interior of a church, having all its pews removed, leaving only the cant pieces on which they were erected, and the spaces between these pieces covered and padded with the beautiful rice-straw matting of the country, you will get a fairly good idea of the simple fittings of a Japanese music hall. A whole family seats itself in one of these squares; and as a concert in this country is really a formidable affair, they bring their braziers, teapots, and chow-boxes with them. The performer—a lady—is seated, tailor fashion, on a raised platform, a music desk in front of her, and her musical instruments near at hand. The Japanese, like the Chinese, sing from the throat, and the effect produced on the tympanum is that of an amorous tom-cat chanting to his lady-love at midnight. The words she is singing, and has been singing for the—a friend who was with me said "*the last week;*" but knowing him to be a joker, I accept the statement with caution—for the last six hours, and which she will probably continue to sing for the next six, contain rather too much levity and grossness, could we understand them, to be at all suitable even for sailors. But her present audience receive them with the utmost indifference, only betraying that they are at all conscious of what is going on by an occasional clapping of the hands. Now and again the singer has a spell and a libation of saki, an attendant keeping her liberally supplied in this item, of which she manages to drink a quantity during her song; and, by way of a change at these times, she enters into a monologue or a recitation. Taken and viewed in an artistic light, the audience in their rich gala dresses is a pleasing piece of color and of harmonic contrasts.

Close to the temple a crowd is gathered around a horse-box, in which is a milk-white steed—sacred, of course. Before him a little table is placed, covered with tiny saucers filled with beans; and the devout—and we in particular—can have the puerile satisfaction of seeing him munch his comfits in a strangely horselike manner for the small sum of a "*sen !*" Near at hand are some more sacred creatures—hundreds of turtles in a slimy pond rear their snake-like heads through the thick green water for the pieces of biscuit and little red balls of prepared food which the children are constantly flinging into their midst. These reptiles, it may be remembered, form an important figure-subject in Japanese carvings, paintings, and bronzes.

Within easy distance of Kobé, and connected with it by rail, are the cities of Osaca and Kioto, the former being the seaport of the latter, and, possibly, the greatest trade centre in the empire. It seems to be built at the delta of a river; and as there are scores of bridges spanning their several mouths, it has much the appearance of Venice. Kioto is the sacred city of Japan, and contains, amongst other interesting sights, a large temple, in which are no fewer than 33,333 gods! Yearly pilgrimages are made here; and to provide spiritual ministrations for the thousands of pilgrims, it is said that the priests form one-fifth of the entire population.

June 17th, to-day we completed with coal and started for Yokohama, leaving the Inland Sea by its south eastern entrance and entering on the broad bosom of the great Pacific. By the help of a splendid breeze we are speedily clear of the Linschoten strait and in view of a strange picture, for giant Fusi begins to rear his hoary head above the main.

At first it appears but a small conical shaped island, rising isolated from the midst of the sea, and which in a few hours we shall reach. But a few hours multiply into scores of hours, and still that island appears at a tantalizing distance, and it is not until the main land comes into view that we discover the misty island is no island at all, but a superb mountain. It can be seen at an immense distance from the sea; we, ourselves, are, at the very least, sixty miles from its base, and yet how clearly distinct, how tangibly present, how boldly out-lined it stands against the opal tints of the evening sky.

Fusi-yama—"the peerless," "the matchless," or "the unrivalled,"—is an extinct volcano, on the island of Niphon, though, only a century since, it was in active operation, and is said to have been brought into existence in the space of a few days, Few sights are likely to leave such an impression on one's mind, as solitary, graceful, cold looking Fusi, which, clothed in a mantle of snow, may, not inaptly, be compared to a grim sentinel guarding the destinies of a nation. But who shall attempt a description of its glories as we saw it that evening at sunset, 'and many an evening afterward, with the chance and transient effect of light and shades playing on its pearly sides.

June 19.—The freshening gale soon rattled us past the town of Simoda, and into the great bay of Yedo, with the volcano of Vries at its entrance. Hundreds of queer-shaped junks and smaller craft, laden with the produce of the busy nation, glide across the rolling seas with duck-like motions, on their peaceful mission to the capital.

I have before had occasion to mention these unintelligible pieces of naval architecture, but as they never before appeared to me at such advantage as now, as they struggle up the wind across our track, I have hitherto refrained from saying much about them. They are constructed very sharp forward and very broad aft, with high, rising sterns something after the manner of the Chinese junk, but far more picturesque and compact than the sister country's vessel; and, so far as looks go, a far more seaworthy craft than the latter. They carry an immense sail of pure white canvas, save where a black cloth is let in—for contrast perhaps—on the huge characters composing the owner's name, mar its fair surface; and a stout, heavy mast placed well abaft the centre of the vessel, and curved at its upper end, the better to form an overhanging derrick to hoist the sail by. The sail is made of any number of cloths laced together vertically—not sewn—by which method each cloth has a bellying property and wrinkled appearance, independent of its neighbours, thus the whole surface holds far more wind than one continuous sheet would do. The vessels, despite their unnautical appearance, sail well on a wind. Some writers have affirmed, that instead of reefing as we do, and as is pretty universal all over the world—namely, by reducing the perpendicular height of the sail—that the Japanese accomplish this by taking in sail *at the sides*, or laterally, by unlacing a cloth at a time. This seems to me highly absurd, and is certainly not borne out by the testimony of my own observation; and that they should not conform to the common usuage of maritime nations—both savage and civilized—in this particular is improbable. Even the Chinese—who are generally admitted to be the most *unconforming* and irrational people in the world—reef their sails, at least, in the orthodox way. Besides taking a practical view of the matter, how are they in any sudden emergency, and with their limited crews, to undo the elaborate lacing, without going out on the yard and climbing *down* the sail, unlacing as they go? So far as I am able to judge, their method is a most simple and effective one, for all that they do is to lower the sail, gather in the slack at the bottom, and as there are several sheets up and down the breech of the sail, the thing is done with the utmost facility.

The build of a junk's stern is somewhat peculiar, for there is a great hollow which, apparently, penetrates the body of the vessel; a mode of construction said to be due to an edict of one of the tycoons, to prevent his subjects from leaving the country; for though it seems incredible, these junks have been known to voyage to India. The sampan has a similar faulty arrangement of stern. Though the people obeyed the spirit of the law, they evaded the letter of it by placing sliding watertight boards across the aperture.

By noon we had anchored off Yokohama, now a large and flourishing town, and the chief naval and foreign trading part of Japan, though, before the English arrived here in 1854, it was little more than a village.

Having got through the noise and smoke of salutes to no less than four admirals, and other minor consular expenditures of gunpowder, we prepared ourselves for a pleasurable stay in the sailor's paradise. Perhaps no place in the round of sailors' visits, certainly none on this station, offers so many inducements, so many and pleasing channels of getting rid of money, as does Yokohama. Certain it is that the officers, who form the banking committee on board, never complain of being over worked, during a ship's stay in this harbour, and plethoric bank books are frequently reduced to a sad and pitiable state of emaciation after having "done" Yokohama and its vicinity.

The residences of the Europeans are situated out of the town on a rising ground to the left, known as the Bluff. Here the merchants live in rural magnificence, each with his mansion surrounded by its own park-like grounds. The English and foreign naval hospitals are also situated in this healthy and beautiful spot; and it was here, too, that our recent marine contingent to Japan had their barrack.

The European concession is a small town in itself, and from the nomenclature of the landing places it would appear that the English and French claim the greatest interests here. These landing stages are called, from the division of the settlement which they front, the English and French "*Hatobahs*"—the "*atter bar*" of the sailor.

As this town is the great point of contest between the Japanese and the foreigner, everything in the shape of "*curios*" can be obtained in its marts and bazaars. Most of the objects are novel to us, and from their attractiveness generally induce sailors to purchase on the strength of that very quality. Except in very rare instances a piece of real lacquer can scarcely be obtained, most of it having already found its way to Europe; that which we see here is made chiefly for sailors, who needs must take something home—they care not what, nor are they very particular about the price asked. And how well these people have studied the "tar;" how they have discovered his weakness for startling colours! I am writing this about four years subsequent to this, our first visit, and one would think, that four years was amply sufficient for the purpose of opening our eyes to deceptions. Have they though? Not a bit of it, for we are quite as ready to be "taken in" to-day or to-morrow, as we were four years since. Still, there are some very handsome and, now and then, really elegant things to be picked up in the shops: bronzes, lacquers, china, tortoise-shell earrings, fans, paintings, or silk, combining in their execution, the most educated taste, and the most wonderful skill. Generally speaking a "Japper" after naming a price will rarely retract. The Chinaman always will, the rogue! The Japanese know this peculiarity of the Chinaman, and nothing will wound a Jap's self-respect more than to compare his mode of dealing with the celestial's.

They seem to enjoy arguing and chaffering over prices, and will frequently go to the length of pulling down masses of paper, supposed to be invoices, to shew that they are asking you fair. We pretend to examine these inventories with a most erudite expression on our ignorant faces, and invariably commence to open the wrong end of the book, forgetful that the Japanese commence at what we call the last page. The dealers display the utmost indifference as to whether you buy or not, and you may pull their shops to pieces without raising their ire in the slightest, for they will bow to you just as ceremoniously on leaving as though you had purchased twenty dollars' worth.

Strange as Japanese art appears to us, there is design in all their executions. This presents a marked contrast to Chinese art, which appears to be simply the result of the artist's fancy. A Chinaman seems to have no idea, when he commences a thing, what he is going to produce, he goes on cutting and scraping, taking advantage of, here a vein in a stone, perhaps, or there a knot in the gnarled branches of a tree, and his imagination, distorted by the diabolical forms with which his superstition surrounds him, does the rest.

* * * * *

And now I will ask you to take a run with me to Tokio, the capital of Japan.

The hour's ride by rail conducts us through a pleasant, well cultivated country. Fields of ripe grain, clusters of woods with cottages peeping out of their bosky shades, and surrounded by stacks of hay and corn, have, for the Englishman, a farm-like and altogether a home-like look.

The best and safest method to adopt on arriving at the terminus is to hire rickshas of the company at the railway station, by so doing you are saved from being victimised by the coolies, who are about as honest as the Jehus of our own streets. You may employ them for as many hours as you please, but to avoid fractions it is usual to engage them by the day.

Until Japan was opened to foreigners, Tokio, or Yedo, was a mystery to the civilized world. It was supposed to be fabulously large, and was said to contain more inhabitants than any other metropolis in the world; some accounts putting it down to as many as four millions. As regards its extent, the city certainly does cover an immense space. Its population, though, is but half that of London. Its large area is due, perhaps, more to the manner in which it is laid out, than to anything else—which is in the form of concentric circles, the mikado's palace, or castle, occupying the centre. Around this dismal, feudal looking, royal abode, the various embassies are erected; buildings which present a far finer—because more modern and European—appearance than does the imperial residence. Circling the whole is a large deep moat, the waters of which are thickly studded with beautiful water lilies, and spanned by several bridges. Then come the dingy and now disused houses and streets of those powerful men of a by-gone age, the daimios. The whole aspect of this question may be summed up in the word *desolation*. This, too, is surrounded by a canal, or moat. Beyond this, again comes the city proper, with its busy, bustling population.

We are entirely at the mercy of our "ricksha" men, and have not the remotest idea of where they are driving us; but assuming they know more about the city than we, this does not exercise us much. They rattle us along over unevenly paved streets, and whiz us around corners with the rapidity of thought; an uncomfortable sensation in the region of the dorsal vertebræ, resulting from the unusual bumping process, and a fear lest, haply, we may be flying out of our carriage at a tangent into somebody's shop front, a pleasing reflection should we take a header amongst china.

Our coolies had been directed to a quarter of the city called Shiba, and here at length we find ourselves, and are shortly set down before one of the grandest buddhist temples in Japan. How peacefully the great building reposes in its dark casket of solemn fir trees! To reach the main entrance, we traverse a broad pathway lined with praying lanterns on either hand. These lanterns are stone pedestals, surmounted by a hollow stone ball with a crescent shaped aperture in its surface, through which, at night, the rays of light proceeding from *burning prayers* penetrate the gloom. Scores of tombs, containing the remains of the defunct tycoons and their wives, fill the temple court; and as each successive tycoon looked forward to reposing here after death, during life he richly embellished it, and endeavoured to make it worthy to receive so august a body as his own.

A bald-headed priest, standing at the great entrance, bids us remove our shoes and follow him. He conducts us up grand stair cases, through corridors, into courtyards, chapels, and sanctuaries; unlocks recesses, and produces sacred vessels of massive gold work of vast antiquity and splendid design, intimating to us that these are for the sole use of the mikado, when he assumes his priestly office. Here we get our first idea of what real lacquer means. Our bonze brought out a small lacquered cubical box, of a dull gold colour, and about four inches in height, and gave us to understand that it could not be purchased for 500 dollars! Just fancy! And then the carving, gilding, colouring, and lacquer, everywhere, is something beyond description. Even the very floors on which we tread, the stairs, the hand-rails, are all gorgeous with vermilion lacquer. One sanctuary is really resplendent, its vessel's mouldings and ornaments being of dead gold work, wrought in all kinds of emblematical designs and shapes. I feel assured that no thoughtful man can visit Shiba's temple without being impressed with the high perfection to which the Japanese have attained in the arts; a perfection which the foreign mind can rarely grasp. After a donation to the polite bonze—which he receives on a gold salver and lays on the altar—we encase our feet in leather once more, and leave the sacred precincts. We may possibly never have the opportunity of paying Shiba a second visit; but the privilege of having done so once is—to a man of research—a liberal education in itself.

The streets and their busy throng are very gay and lively. Hosts of healthy-looking and prettily clad children are running here, there, and everywhere in pursuit of their kites, and other childish amusements. Vendors hawking their wares, as at home; the shrill melancholy whistle of the blind shampooer who, with a staff in one hand and a short bamboo pipe in the other, thus apprises people of his willingness to attend on them; ladies bowing and "sayonaraing" each other in musical tones; the encouraging voice of the driver to his jaded ox; and the warning "a—a" of the *ricksha* man; these are the music of the streets in "the land of the rising sun."

The city can boast in the possession of several very fine and extensive parks, that in which the Naval College is situate being one of the largest. Here the youthful Japanese officers of the navy were educated by English instructors in all the branches and requirements of the modern naval service, and some of the work we saw in the different parts of the building shews that the Japanese have become thorough masters of the technicalities, and no mean adepts at their practical application. All the foreign instructors—except one—have now been discharged, the Japanese feeling themselves strong enough to walk alone in naval matters. That one exception is a chief gunner's mate, who so rarely uses the English language that, on conversing with us, he had frequently to pause to consider what words he should make use of, and even then his English was broken, and spoken just as a native would speak it.

On the return ride to Yokohama I was fortunate enough to find myself seated next a gentleman who has been resident in Japan upwards of twenty-five years, during which period he has travelled throughout the length and breadth of the empire. As may be imagined he was a repository of much valuable and varied information. He could hoist out facts and figures as easily as you would fling a weevily biscuit to leeward. From his conversation with me I gained much knowledge about Japan, which it was impossible I could have acquired in any other way, and all of which I have embodied in various parts of this narrative.

The manner in which the natural taste is assimilating itself to European ideas appears more evident when one comes to observe the hundreds of Japanese who take advantage of the railway. Stop at what station you like, you will find the platform suddenly alive with gaily dressed and clogged passengers, on pleasure bent, loaded with toys or wares that have been purchased in the gay capital.

A few days after the above events the Japanese squadron

of smart corvettes, and the large ironclad "Foo-soo" (Great Japan, as we say Great Britain,) got under way and proceeded to sea. It was rumoured that the mikado was to have accompanied in his yacht, and in anticipation of his embarkation all the men-of-war in harbour dressed ship, though, as it turned out, he did not put in an appearance.

July 3rd.—General Grant arrived this morning in the corvette "Richmond," and escorted by a Japanese man-of-war. All ships, except the English and German, dressed in honour of the American flag, which the corvette flew at her main. The two nationalites I have mentioned seem to have offered a marked discourtesy to the general, the German especially so, for just as the "Richmond" was about to anchor the "Prinz Adalbert" broke the German royal standard at her royal mast head, which, as it were, blew the charges out of guns already loaded for the American. The "Adalbert" has Prince Heinrich, the second son of our Princess Royal, on board as a midshipman; hence the standard.

It would appear that the slight passed on Jonathan did not go entirely unnoticed by him, for in the evening, at sunset, when, as is customary with that nation, her band played her colours down and then the national anthems, it was noticed that the English and German tunes were studiously omitted.

But the "Richmond" had taken up a bad billet to anchor in, and to find a more secure one she steamed out to the entrance of the harbour and made a wide sweep before returning. Some of our jocular shipmates had quite a different view of this proceeding, for, if we are to

I

believe them, the American went out to take the turn out of her flags, or to allow her ship's company to bathe, the waters of the harbour being too shallow for the latter purpose!

Unwillingly my pen has once again to trace the lines which are to record the death of another of our poor fellows, Frederick Smyth, a stoker. Returning from leave in one of the open, dangerous, shallow boats of the place, and perhaps slightly the worse for liquor, the unfortunate man fell overboard, his body not being recovered until some days after the sad event.

July 22nd.—Up anchor once more! Onward is our motto, nor are we particularly sorry to be on the move, for I think everybody is surfeited with Yokohama, and perhaps the fact that everybody's money is all gone, has something to do with our eagerness to be off. So, boys, "We'll go to sea for more," as the old tars did. Just as the anchor was a-trip two royal personages came on board, the Princes Arisugawa—father and son; the father being the commander-in-chief of the Japanese army; the son a "midshipmite" in the Imperial navy. They were attended by their suite and Sir Harry Parkes, the British ambassador at Tokio. We took them a short distance to sea with us, and after seeing one or two evolutions they returned to Yokohama in the "Vigilant," whilst we resumed our voyage.

CHAPTER XI.

*From clime to clime, from sea to sea, we roam,
'Tis one to us—we head not yet for home.*

NORTHWARD—HAKODADI—DUI—CASTRIES BAY—
BARRACOUTA—VLADIVOSTOCK.

SHORTLY after rounding Mela Head and shaping our course to the northward, the temperature underwent a marked change, in fact so suddenly were we ushered into a colder zone that everybody is on the search for pocket handkerchiefs, these articles being in very general demand.

The eastern coast of Niphon, along which we are now cruising, has several admirable harbours and sheltered anchorages. Two days after leaving Yokohama we found the ship standing in for the land and making for Yamada, one of the securest harbours on the coast. Bold hills and headlands, clothed in the easily recognisable dark green foliage of the fir, rear themselves on either hand as we pass into the outer bay. This outer sheet of water—for there is an inner—has a very broad opening seaward, but suddenly, on changing course, a narrow inlet reveals a noble bay, perfectly land-locked with a village of considerable size at its head. No sooner had our anchor left the bows than a volunteer party asked and obtained permission to go fishing. So far, however, as catching fish was concerned, the expedition was a signal failure, though, looked at in the light of enjoyment, it was a perfect success. Along the beach of this arcadia an abundance of flowers grow in a wild state, amongst them the rose, whose beauty, bloom, and fragrance equalled those of the choicest culture in our English garden; and on looking at them and the other familiar flowers around, we might have been forgiven for fancying ourselves at home. Whence come our associates, and why is it that even the fragrance of a flower is capable of seizing hold on the mind, and transporting it to the utmost limits of a continent?

The usual wondering throng of natives speedily gathered around us, eager to participate in the viands which we were endeavouring to stow away. Fortunately we had plenty of biscuit with which to satisfy their curiosity; but it was a long time before they could be prevailed upon to drink out of a basin of cocoa. When we offered it to them they touched their heads and swayed their bodies to and fro, making a very creditable pantomime of intoxication. At length, however, one of us used the Japanese word "*tcha*" (tea) which had the desired effect, for one man advanced, took a drink, and liked it; and though he of course discovered it was not tea, he also found out it was not rum.

July 27th—We have now reached the northern end of Niphon, and turned westward into the broad strait of

Tsugar, which separates the greater island from Yesso. The scenery about the strait is very lovely; all day we have coasted the land down, and alternate hill and dale, and here and there a giant volcano peak were most refreshing objects on which to rest the eye. Towards evening the great open bay of Awomori came into view, and in a short time we had entered it, and cast anchor opposite a small town, built on a level grassy plain. The irregularly scattered houses, amidst trees and greensward, have something the appearance of Singapore, when viewed from the seaward.

Our stay was but short, for on the following morning our anchor was at the bows, and the ships heading for Hakodadi. This town—the largest in Yesso—reminds one very forcibly of Gibraltar. There is a similar high rock standing sheer out of the sea—almost the same narrow strip of land connecting it with the main; whilst the town is built on the slopes of the eminence, and circling the bay as at Gib. The town is not over large, and commodities are very scarce, the only thing obtainable being dried salmon.

During our stay the ship's company landed under arms — a by no means pleasurable treat, as you shall see. The waters near the shore were so shallow that the men experienced great difficulty in reaching the beach, and were only able to accomplish it after wading through about twenty yards of mud and water, dragging guns and ammunition with them. Add to this the inconvenience of drilling and marching in dripping clothes, and the knowledge that the same performance must be repeated to embark again; and you will see that a sailor's life is not all sugar. Hakodadi is not a place that sailors are likely to fall in love with, for there is no accommodation on shore for them; yet leave was given, and the men had to "bunk it out" where they could. On this occasion—let me record it in the reddest of red letters, or in the most emphatic italics—*a liberty boat was granted.*

August 3rd—To-day is Sunday, and a sort of preliminary inspection by the admiral, but—would you believe it?—he completely ignored the beautifully cleaned deck and stanchions, the glistening whitewash, and all the other aids to appearances, well known to sailors, and put on specially for the occasion! Yes, he actually took not the slightest notice of these, but, instead, poked his head into all the holes and corners where he was likely to find sundry and various small gear, such as dirty towels, "duff" bags, ditty bags, and so forth. The result might have been anticipated. He turned out so much that, before he had gone a third of the way around the lower deck, he gave the captain orders to make a personal inspection first, and then report to him; and as everyone knows, when once Captain Cleveland gets into that canvas suit of his, he is —in naval phrase—"a dead rivet."

One night, as we lay here ready for sea, a man-of-war was observed entering the harbour, and as soon as the flashing lights were brought to bear, and her number made, she proved to be the "Charybdis," last from Yokohama. She informed us that, subsequent to her leaving that port, cholera had broken out amongst her crew, one man having died of it on the passage, whilst a second was down with the disease, though he was now in a fair way towards recovery. She was at once ordered into quarantine, and to hoist the " yellow jack " at the fore. Young Prince Arisugawa was also on board, taking passage to join our ship as naval cadet ; however, he was not permitted to come to us until he had been overhauled by the doctors on shore, and his clothes fumigated. Immediately he had left her the "Charybdis" was ordered to sea ; the bracing sea air of a more northern clime being about the most effective medicine for her crew.

August 9.—To-day Prince Arisugawa came on board, and in due course was consigned to the tender mercies of the young English gentlemen in the gunroom ; his future messmates—and shall I be wrong if I say *tormentors?* At the same time a most acceptable gift to the ship's company, consisting of eight bullocks, was brought alongside ; the present, I believe, of the Emperor, whose health we *ate* next day.

Steam was already up when the prince embarked, and there was nothing further to detain us except the weather. That, indeed, was very threatening, and not to be ignored. Terrific peals of thunder and blinding lightning, accompanied by such heavy and persisted showers of rain that it was a mystery how the soil could withstand such an inundation, delayed our sailing for upwards of four hours. At the end of that time nature again resumed her wonted smiling appearance, the sun chasing away such evidences of bad temper with the rapidity of thought.

Nothing of moment occurred on our voyage up the gulf of Tartary, except that, during one middle watch, the ship narrowly escaped running on a rock ; but as she did not actually touch, we verify the adage that " a miss is as good as a mile." The day following, the lifting of a fog-bank revealed to us the "Charybdis" close in shore, under small sail. On signalling us that she had pitched her late unwelcome visitor overboard, she was allowed to join company, and afterwards proceeded on to Dui, to coal and order some for us.

August 13th.—Sad misfortune! direful calamity! Why? Read, and you will be as wise as myself. In the middle watch of this night, our two cats—have I told you that we brought two cats from England with us?—as was their wont, were skylarking and cutting capers on the hammock nettings and davits, when tabby the lesser, instead of jumping on something palpable, made a leap on space with the natural result, for he lighted on water and was rapidly whirled astern by the inky waters of the Tartar gulf. Poor pussy, little did we dream, or you either, that Siberian waters were to sing your requiem! We feel very sorry at the loss of our pet, for he was a thorough sailor, thinking it nothing to mount the rigging and seat himself on the crosstrees, whilst on his rounds; and as to the item "rats," shew me the rodent that could ever boast of weathering him, and I will shew you a clever beast.

At daybreak we made the harbour of Dui, in the island of Saghalien, a Russian penal settlement and coaling depôt, though coaling is under such severe restrictions that the trouble to secure it is worth its cost. For instance, only a certain number of tons can be had each day, and then only for one ship at a time; and instead of using large lighters to bring it off, small boats are employed, rendering it necessary to make a multiplicity of visits to the shore. This island, until recently a part of the Japanese empire, is rich in coal, and other minerals, a fact Russia was careful to note when casting her covetous eyes over its broad surface.

It may be remembered, perhaps, that in the year 1879, Russia sent her first batch of Nihilists and other political offenders to Siberia, by the more expeditious sea route, and that alarming reports had crept into the European press, and especially into that of the national censor, the English, as to the cruelties and inhumanities these poor people had to endure on the voyage. The vessel, with the convicts on board, was lying at Dui on our arrival, and our admiral was not slow to avail himself of the means of satisfying himself, and, through him, the English press, as to the alleged enormities. He found, I believe, that far from being badly treated, the prisoners had every consideration allowed them consistent with their position as state prisoners. Indeed, the convicts on this island seem to enjoy almost perfect liberty of action, short of being permitted to escape, for I encountered about a score of them 'on shore—big, burly, well-fed fellows—smoking, playing at pitch-and-toss, and singing, as if to be a convict was a state to be desired rather than otherwise. Possibly, these were good characters, for I certainly saw some in the coaling hulks with heavy chains on their wrists and legs, and with half-shaved heads—a distinguishing mark which those I met on shore had not.

By dint of extra pressure we managed to procure our coal next day, though it took us till after sundown to get in 140 tons. We and the "Charybdis" then sailed—she for Yokohama and we for Castries bay—about sixty miles on the other side of the gulf—where we dropped anchor on the following morning.

We felt the weather bitterly cold, as contrasted with the temperature of our experience since leaving England, though, I suppose, at home such would be called genial.

There is not a sign or semblance of the human species, near this spot. All around us is forest, forest to the utmost limit of vision. Pines and firs, firs and pines, for acres upon acres; sufficient, I should think, to furnish all the navies of the world, present and yet unborn, with spars. What a solemn and wintry aspect these northern forests have; what weird murmurs and ghostly sighs haunt their virgin glades. Sometimes in the midst of this almost black greenness, some forest monarch, bleached and scared by the icy breath of generations of Siberian winters, stands out with skeleton distinctness. A dreary, desolate place altogether. There must be a town somewhere in the vicinity, though, for in the afternoon the military commandant hove in sight. This official had on the enormous bearskin head-dress, and dark green uniform of the Cossack regiment. An insignificant-looking man, all moustache and swagger.

On Monday, the day following our arrival, to all those who cared to avail themselves of it, a regular day's outing was granted. We started early, so as to have a long day before us. We had permission to fish to our heart's content, in waters where fish is specially abundant and good. It was rather a long pull to the shore, and shallow water there when we reached it, for we had gone a considerable distance up a small river. The town (so it is called) of Alexandrovsk—at the same time the village of "Tighee" (Torpoint) would make four such towns—was passed on our way up. We pushed on into the interior as far as we could drag our larger boats, and selected our encampment on a spit of beach, near the dwellings of some natives. These huts were of tent shape and constructed of bark, and covered with the skins of the reindeer, numbers of which animals we can see grazing in the vicinity.

The inhabitants of this little-known part of the great asiatic continent, are mongolian Tartars. They are possessed of a rather forbidding cast of feature, have great square, flat faces, the nose scarcely distinguishable, and swallowed up in the flattening process (this though, by the way, is an index of beauty amongst them), low foreheads, and dreamy-looking obliquely-set eyes. Their head-gear is much after the Chinese style, except, that in addition to the queue, they allow the remainder of the hair to develop itself, which it does in the wildest and most elfish manner. For dress, the untanned skins of the animals caught in the chase, with the hair outboard, answers all their requirements. At first one experiences a great difficulty in distinguishing the sexes, for the ordinary bearings by which we sight " danger " ahead are entirely wanting. Stay, are they *all* absent? Scarcely, for the vanity inherent in woman displays itself even here. These ladies have large *iron* rings in their ears, and through the cartilage of the nose a similar pendant is hung, on which is an additional ornament of a green stone, much resembling the mineral malachite. Their dress is a very capacious, continuous garment of the yellow skin of the hair seal, seamed with sinews, and very rudely put together. Hundreds of yelping dogs lay about in all possible attitudes of laziness, whilst a few other village pets, *e.g.*, a great bald-headed eagle, of a most bloodthirsty and ferocious aspect, and a couple of large brown bears with uncomfortable looking teeth and arms, suggestive of a long embrace, stood unpleasantly near, though their owners had thought fit to secure them.

This people's religion is a strange mixture of heathenism and Greek church Christianity. The czar's soldiers have a very short and effective manner of converting the subjugated races which bow before their swords, by driving the whole batch at the point of the bayonet into the nearest stream, whilst a little Greek cross is put round the neck of each, and a copy of the bible given them. Near these huts I observed an idol of the rudest construction. It was supposed, I presume, to represent a man's shape—but it was merely a flat board, with the lower end sharpened to a point to fix in the ground, and the upper end fashioned into a very ambiguous circle to form a head; the mouth, nose, and eyes being afterwards added in pigment. One old gent pulled from some obscure retreat in the internal structure of his ample ulster, a pocket edition of the Acts of the Apostles, in English, and from the careful manner in which it was preserved, and the security of its hiding place, he seemed to set great store by it. I tried to surmise how such a volume could have come into his possession, and could only account for it by supposing it had washed up on the beach; but then, if so, why such reverential care of the book. Missionaries, say you. Well, a missionary would scarcely provide himself with copies of the English scripture for distribution amongst gilyaks and calmuck Tartars.

Meanwhile our fishers had pushed on still further inland, dragging the dingy after them, and had met with such success that they returned to camp with their boat laden to the gunwale with salmon and salmon trout. But of all the fish taken that day, by far the finest specimen was that captured near the camping ground. This was a magnificent salmon, of over forty pounds weight, that had become entangled in the long grass with which the surface of the river was covered, a circumstance which rendered him an easy prey to his enemies.

Resuming our southward voyage, our next place of call was Barracouta harbour. It was here, if I am rightly informed, that a French naval officer shot himself, because he had allowed the Russian squadron to overreach him. It was during the Crimean war, the English and French squadrons had hunted the station all over to come up with the Russians, but though they often sighted the enemy, they never succeeded in engaging them. From China to Japan, from Japan to Corea, and away in Siberian waters, it was all the same; the Russians were perfectly successful in out manœuvring their enemy. At length the squadron was again sighted, and their capture seemed a dead certainty, when suddenly it disappeared into a small inlet, apparently in the iron-bound coast of Kamtschatka. Without charts, or the remotest knowledge of the locality, it would be madness to follow. The British, indeed, did manage to find their way into Petropoloski, and succeeded, I believe, in setting fire to one old hulk. It was a most inglorious business throughout, and so worked on the exciteable temperament of the French commanding officer, that he decided to die by his own hand rather than survive such a questionable victory.

On entering the harbour we observed the " Pegasus " at

anchor, seemingly in a wilderness of fir trees. This is the first time we have seen this smart little sloop, as she is a recent addition to our fleet.

There is an abundance of wild fruits here; the raspberries, in particular, being specially fine in size, and delicious in flavour. These and sloes were the only two we recognised, and we took especial care to go in for none of the others; wisely deciding that it was better to confine ourselves to the known. After traversing a virgin forest—soft, mossy, and velvety to the naked feet—and now and again wading muddy streams, studded with artificial islets, composed of roots and other *debris*—in fact floating islands—we at length came out into a clearing, in which was a collection of huts, and a number of women engaged in the preparation of fish, but for what purpose I am to this day ignorant. The manner in which they set about their work is most revolting. Unpleasant though I know it will look in print, nevertheless it must be described. Each woman is armed with a sharp, crescent-shaped blade—seemingly of steel—with which she makes an incision in the back of the neck of the fish, sufficiently deep to penetrate the skin; then taking the animal in both her hands, and applying her teeth to the wound, she tears a long strip off towards the tail, which disappears down her throat with the rapidity and movements of an eel, or of macaroni " down the neck " of a Neapolitan beggar. This, I presume, is called the tit-bit, for the remainder is thrown on one side into a pit, amongst a heap of putrid, festering fish, to undergo the rotting process, necessary to a perfect cure. The appetite of these squaws seem unsatiable; for during the short time we looked on, three of them managed to get outside of about twenty salmon trout, in this manner.

After a stay of three days in this pretty little spot, we started, under very unfavourable circumstances. The weather was very cold and foggy, and rain fell in abundance, so altogether it was very unpleasant. But this was not all, for on making the open sea the wind began to rise, and we close to a lee shore. We speedily prepared for a gale, as night was coming on, and no indications of the wind going down. The "Pegasus" was still in company; and the two ships kept up a pretty lively conversation with each other during that night of fog, by means of that nautical toy, the steam whistle. Fast and furious they went at it, singing sweet lullabys to the slumbering tars of the watch below. Such horrible shrieks and appalling yells would startle a Red-Indian war-whoop into fits. I feel certain, from subsequent remarks on the subject—let fall in the manner peculiar to seamen—that if their wishes had been answered that night, all the waters in the sea would not have been sufficient to cool the place where they would have consigned the whole apparatus.

At daybreak, the little patch of blue up aloft that mariners so delight to see, shewed us hopes of a fine day. Shortly afterwards we observed a Russian corvette standing out from the land, having just left the anchorage we are about to visit, namely, Olga bay, another fine harbour on the Siberian seaboard. Here we found the Russian admiral, the "Vigilant," and an Italian frigate—the "Vittor Pisani." From hence the "Pegasus" was despatched to Nagasaki, whilst we and the "Vigilant" headed for Vladivostock, calling at Nayedznik bay on the way, and anchoring for the night.

We made three or four attempts to start in the morning, but each time were compelled to delay our departure, out of respect for the heavy fogs which would gather so rapidly in our vicinity. When at length we did get outside, things did not improve, by which we infer that the maritime region of Siberia is a dangerous one at this season. However we steamed along at a pretty brisk rate, and by 10 a.m. had the satisfaction of seeing Vladivostock open out before us. This town is Russia's principal seaport and naval station in this part of her dominions—the head quarters of her navy, and the great military depôt. It has an extremely pleasant appearance from the harbour. On going on shore, though, and examining things in detail I saw that the houses which looked so charming from the ship were constructed of rough unhewn logs of timber, the crevices being filled up with mud. The inhabitants are principally Russian, of course—soldiers and sailors, with their wives; but, in addition, there are Coreans, Chinese, and a few (very few) Japanese. The Russian women are coarse and masculine in appearance, are dressed in cotton print gowns put on very slovenly, wear no covering on the head except their unkempt and dishevelled hair, ride on horseback like a man, and have their feet and legs encased in enormous sea-boots. Everybody wears these leather boots just as everyoné is an equestrian. Even the officers' wives have a slovenly, faded look; and I can honestly say that I never saw one amongst them whom, from her appearance, I should style a lady. There is scarcely a street or road in the place, and the only thoroughfare is that suggested by the deep and sloppy ruts made by the heavy lumbering cart and the uncomfortable *drosky*—the latter a four-wheeled concern peculiar to Russia, possessing a couple of seats running fore and aft, and so near the ground that the passengers' feet are in imminent danger of being brought in contact with stray stones and other inequalities.

In a town such as this one would expect to find commodities both reasonable in price and plenty in variety. Not so, however; what little business there is in the provision line is in the hands of the "ubiquitous"—I mean the Chinaman. Lemonade is a thing unknown, and none of us was bold enough to tackle that vile brew—Russian beer. Of course, like all salt water fish, after being on shore for a short time we wanted "damping;" but there seemed no possibility of our wants being understood, as, seemingly, nobody could speak English. Now, when the British seaman particularly wants anything to drink, and can't get it, he generally uses language which (all things considered) is rather more forcible than polite—that is to say, we would not care for ladies to hear it. It was so here. Vladivostock was this, that, and the other, garnished with sundry and manifold adjectives; in fact it was anything but a town. I dare say, had our sailors the least inkling that all this while they were listened to and understood, they would have reserved some of their more choice figures of speech. It was so, however; for suddenly somebody asked, in splendid English, "Do you require anything, gentlemen?" Our interrogator was a Russian military officer, with several ribbons and crosses on his broad breast. We stated our difficulty, and he very politely directed us to a French hotel, and even accompanied us part of the way. I certainly was not prepared to hear English spoken so well by a Rooski.

K

CHAPTER XII.

"Come, friends, who plough the sea,
A truce to navigation, let's take another station."

CHEFOO—NAGASAKI EN ROUTE.—JAPAN REVISITED.—
KOBE.—YOKOHAMA.

AUGUST 31st.—At the early hour of four this morning the shrill sound of those ear-piercing instruments, the boatswains' pipes in combination, resounded clearly and distinctly in the pure raw air, as "all hands" summoned the sleepy crew to heave up anchor. In less than an hour, thanks to the modern sailors' help, the steam capstan, our white wings were spread for the expected breeze outside the harbour. As yet, however, the wind has not been enticed, it being, as one of our shipmates from the sister isle put it, "a dead calm, with what wind there was dead ahead." Further on we overhauled a splendid breeze, which caused our canvas to strain in every fibre as we careened to its pressure. This gave us such material help that by noon of next day we had carved a good big slice out of the six hundred miles to Nagasaki.

September 3rd.—From the greasy appearance of the moon last night, and from a study of other varied phenomena whereby sailors, from time immemorial, have learnt to forecast the weather, we "smelt" a change of some sort was about to happen; and we sleepers, on turning out in the morning, were in no wise surprised to find that the wind had headed us, that all the sails were furled, and the ship poking her nose into a nasty sea. But this was a blind: the clerk of the weather was evidently meditating a stronger blow from the original direction, and had only gone on ahead to seek some of his refractory forces to give us the full benefit of the combination. All sail again, fast and furious we drove through it, and succeeded in knocking "seven and a bit" out of the old "Duke;" 'twould take something like a hurricane to persuade her to more. We tore past Tsu-sima, an island in the Corea strait, and laughingly cleared the run down to Nagasaki.

September 4th.—As information had reached us at Vladivostock that cholera was raging pretty freely at Nagasaki, instead of proceeding at once to the anchorage we brought up at the mouth of the harbour, under the lee of Tacabuco, until such times as we should hear more definite and accurate accounts of the extent of the enemy's depredations. Like another much-libelled personage, who is often painted much blacker than he perhaps is, the cholera, through undoubtedly present, was confined to the poorer haunts of the city, so that with necessary precautions there was nothing to fear. Stopping everybody's leave, though, unfortunately happened to be a necessary precaution, and communication with the shore was limited to the visits of the bumboat and washermen.

On the following morning we commenced to fill up with coal. I have before remarked that in this port we have lady coal heavers. It so chanced that for once they were rather short-handed, and to expedite the work a party of blue-jackets were sent to clear a spare lighter. Whether or not they mistook the commander's order, or whether their eyes had got blinded with coal dust I can't say, but sure am I that they failed, every man-jack of them, to go into the indicated boat. May be, the sight of women at "unwomanly work" was too much for Jack's chivalry—at any rate, they had jumped in among the women and were cheerfully heaving out the coal whilst the latter had a smoke. Now this, however laudable in itself, was clearly not the commander's intention, and the gallants, much against their will, had to yield to pressure and clear the bachelor lighter.

September 7th.—In company with the "Growler" and "Sylvia" we left the shores of fair Nagasaki; and after despatching the small fry about their business we shaped our course for Chefoo. The wind for a short distance was again fair; but having, presumably, discovered its mistake, and that we had had a full share of his favors lately, old boisterous suddenly changed his tactics, and intimated to us in unmistakable language, by alternate lulls and squalls, that he was about to do something rash. At noon of the second day out, after, we must confess, ample warning, he had apparently decided what to do, the wind came up as foul as it could well be. We were at this time off the island of Quelpart, still carrying reduced sail and barely going our course.

The breeze, though strong, was steady and all went well until the ship reached the western extremity of the mountainous island, when, with a roar and a screech truly terrific, a squall struck us in wild, fitful gusts. We were carrying reefed topsails and trysails at the time, and it was fortunate that we had no more sail on, or surely our spars must have gone over the side. As it was, the fore trysail split with the report of a cannon, and the main-topsail, unable to stand the enormous strain, was torn from top to bottom. To make things more cheerful, the clouds, in their sport, hurled blinding slanting sheets of water at us; for it would be an error to say that rain fell. An effort was made to furl sails; but though there was no lack of cheerful hands speedily on the yards, numbers became powerless to manipulate canvas which by the combined elements had been converted into deal boards. As it was impossible that orders could be heard from deck, the officers went aloft and lay out on the yards amongst the men, encouraging them by voice and example. The attempt had to be given up and the sails secured to the yards by lashings.

September 11th.—The dreary, monotonous, unenlivening coast line of China, with its interminable sand hills and granite peaks, once more in sight. The landscapes of north China are, if anything, more dreary than ever. We must however take the bad with the good. Chefoo lies before us, and into Chefoo we are bound to go. We cannot, as yet, see any town, because of a sort of natural breakwater of sand and rocks which stretches almost across the harbour's mouth; but that there is an anchorage beyond is clear, from the thousands of masts pointing skyward. So slow was our progress into the harbour that it seemed as if we were never going to get there at all; but eventually we dropped anchor at about three miles from what I suppose pretends to be a town, but which from such a distance looked more like a straggling village. We had gone in quite far enough, though, for every revolution of the screws discoloured the water with sand and mud, and, furthermore, I believe we touched, for a distinct not to be mistaken vibration was clearly felt by all hands. This part of the anchorage is much exposed to the sea; and, in the event of a blow from the northward, we are in a position to encounter its full fury. Chefoo, notwithstanding its uninteresting appearance, seems to be a pretty regular port of call for men-of-war, several of which are lying at anchor within the bar.

There must be some spots in the neighbourhood capable of cultivation, for our bumboat is loaded with an abundance of tempting fruits—grapes of rich bloom and large growth, apples which would do no discredit to a West of England orchard, and peaches scarcely inferior to those of the Mediterranean. And how cheap everything is—eggs you can get for the asking almost, whilst a whole fowl (prepared and cooked in a manner which, out of charity to the Chinese culinary art, we wont pry into too closely, but which our sailor gourmands relish nevertheless) is obtainable for five cents! I infer, of course, to that bird which our shipmates denominate "*dungaree chicken.*" Our first impression of Chefoo is that it is the place of all others on the station to send emaciated ships' companies to regain their stamina.

The district has a special manufacture of silk, much

prized by our female friends at home, made from the fibres of the bamboo. Did you ever see such a wonderful plant as that same bamboo? I could not enumerate half the uses to which the natives of China and Japan apply its beautiful slender golden stem. The silk, of a color resembling brown holland, is really very good, and makes excellent summer out-door dresses for the European ladies and girls at Chefoo. Some of the best costumes I noticed on shore were made of this material.

Shortly after our arrival the "Vigilant" came in, en route for Tientsin, a port further up the Gulf of Pe-chili, and to the westward of us. You may perhaps remember that it was here the recent massacre of some helpless French sisters of mercy took place, an event which at one time seemed very likely to have embroiled China into a war with France.

I wonder if I should be wrong in saying that one of the principal reasons which makes this so desirable a port for navy ships is the advantages presented by the sand-bar at the mouth of the harbour for shore evolutions? This may or may not be so; but scarcely a week passed without our captain taking us ashore to play at soldiers, and sometimes two or even three times a week. The bar has many qualities suitable for military operations; a rocky grass-covered mound at the western extremity in particular forming an excellent position for the field guns and assaulting parties. This spot will be always remembered by our ship's company by the name of Fort Cleveland, a name they themselves bestowed on it, because the captain, who conducted these landing parties with strict regard to military tactics, so frequently made it the culminating point in the day's manœuvres.

After all it was deemed advisable to shift out of our present unsafe anchorage to a more secure one inside the bar, and, as the "Modeste" was about to leave for Chusan, she came alongside and took us in tow. We have met with no heavy weather here yet; but we shall be fortunate indeed if we don't get a "brew" at this season.

We had been here somewhere about ten days when the Chinese governor came on board, attended, as is the custom in China, by a numerous suite of lesser mandarins and their retainers. Chefoo is an important military command, as well as one of the chief naval ports in the empire; hence the governor is a high military mandarin. From the governor downwards they were all dressed pretty much alike. The mandarins were distinguishable only by a button, worn on the top of their mushroom hats. The colour and material of this button, like the "tails" of a pasha, indicate the position of the wearer, the red being considered the highest of all. In addition to the button the military insignia of a tuft of horse hair, dyed scarlet, depended from the top of the hat of each, whilst some of the more fortunate wore a peacock's feather stuck jauntily under the button. I say more fortunate because, like our K.C.B.'s, only a very few can ever hope to attain to such a mark of the sovereign's favor. These feathers are bestowed by the emperor, generally in person, on such of his subjects as have achieved some renown, either as a soldier or in the equally honorable province of letters. We may well believe, then, that amongst such a people as the Chinese, whose very breath almost is at the emperor's pleasure, such a distinction is the chiefest ambition of every man; for *all* may aspire to it.

A day or so subsequent to the events I have described before, the captain of a trading junk from Tientsin reported that the "Vigilant" had grounded in the Pei-ho, and had sustained considerable damage to her rudder and stern-post, a report which was strictly true; for soon the admiral returned, and at once ordered the "Vigilant" to Hong Kong for repairs.

Shortly before sailing the admiral inspected the ship. On this occasion "Sailor," our widowed cat, was decked out in all the gay and gaudy trappings of a field officer on parade, and, what is more to the point, he was seemingly quite aware that he was looking smart. I suppose "Sailor" can never have read the "Jackdaw of Rheims," but he certainly *looked* the words of that conceited bird as he strutted proudly along before the admiral; and I feel assured that, though the commander-in-chief may not have thought much about the matter, there was no doubt in pussy's mind as to *his* being one of the "greatest folk here to-day."

By the third day out we had reached the Corean archipelago, and found ourselves off the northern coast of Quelpart, where we had recently met with such rough handling. The course was slightly altered to enable us to touch at a small island in the same group, named Port Hamilton. This, until very recently, was, I believe, the only place in the peninsula empire where foreigners— Europeans and Americans—were allowed to hold any intercourse with the natives. It was left to our admiral to alter this edict, and to break through their prejudices.

October 23rd.—At four o'clock this morning we dashed through the strait of Simoneski under steam and canvas, with the wind dead aft and fresh, in company with some hundreds of junks, whose bellying snowy sails and neat trim hulls had much the appearance of a yachting contest.

By sundown we had made the original anchorage. Owing, I suppose, to the season being further advanced, the scenery has lost that freshness we noticed during our first trip through, but not its charm—I think it could never do that. The little bay looked very lovely to-night with the moon's flood of silver light streaming down on its thousand isles.

"Fair luna" had scarcely left us to gladden another world of night before the anchor was at the bows and the ship holding on her onward course; and though the wind was both strong and favourable, no advantage was taken of it to sail, for we were navigating such intricate labyrinths, cutting so sharply around islets, and dodging in and out so many channels and passages, that the jib and spanker were the only sails that could be used with any degree of safety; but when at length we broke out into the open again, we spread our wings to the gale and made short work of the distance to Kobé.

Our arrival was most opportune, both for ourselves and also for society on shore. To the regatta committee we were specially welcome, for a regatta was to be held in the afternoon, and the presence of our band was certainly a pleasing and unlooked-for item in the programme of proceedings. Our third cutter took the first prize in the navy race, though it was an open question whether the Russian boat did not deserve it. It was ruled that "Rooski" had forfeited all claim to a place, in consequence of fouling twice—so somebody said; though there were others who declared that ours fouled the Russians. This led to angry words, and a considerable show of splenetic feeling amongst the committee, which was at length toned down by the appearance of a Russian officer, who begged that, rightly or wrongly, the prize might be awarded to the English boat.

Whilst at Kobé an event took place on board, of small moment indeed to the big outside world, but one of considerable interest amongst ourselves, namely, the birth of a lamb. If we except the rats and cockroaches, and a few such-like atomies, this is the first being which has drawn its first breath on board. One of the sheep taken in at Chefoo happened to be in an "interesting condition," and as nature was not to be thwarted of her purpose by big guns and tarry sailors, the little fellow came along in due course. We are anxious that he may live, for it is wonderful what tricks and antics sailors can train a lamb to, not the least being the avidity with which, after a few lessons, he makes his number at the grog tub at the sound of the bugle.

November 3rd.—Onward, ever onward; a flying visit to Yokohama, and then back home again, or the nearest approach to home that this part of the world affords for Englishmen.

But how changed is Yokohama now! Dirty, wet, cold, and dreary, and all the other adjectives by which discomfort is usually interpreted. During our stay our negro troupe came prominently before the public. At the request of the managing committee of the Temperance Hall the captain yielded, a somewhat reluctant assent, to the attendance of the troupe. They performed before a highly pleased and encouraging audience, and had no occasion to blush at the report of the entertainment in the papers. At any rate many a disinterested resident in the cause of temperance was induced to unbutton his pockets to further that end.

An entertainment, on a vastly different scale, was given to our officers, by the imperial family at Tokio. For a whole day they were the guests of Prince Arisugawa in his capacity of heir-apparent to the royal dignities. Perhaps "heir-apparent" is not strictly the correct term to apply to the royal "mid," the emperor having the power to bestow the crown on whomsoever he lists at his demise. The prince is but the adopted son of the emperor, who has issue of his own; he may set aside, and it is generally understood that he will do so, his own children in favour of his adopted child; by no means an uncommon custom amongst the nobility of Japan.

Recent arrivals from the southward having reported stormy passage, more than the usual precautions were taken to prepare the ship for whatever might chance to fall athwart our hawse. A deck cargo of coals was taken in, storm sails bent, extra gripes put on the boats, and anchors lashed; but, as generally turns out in such cases, neither of these preparations were more than ordinary necessary, for save a roll or two in Formosa's tumbling channel, the splitting of a stunsail boom, and the snapping of a rope now and then, the passage was a fairly smooth one. We put in at Matson, en route, when we found the "Lapwing" awaiting our arrival with mails and the men we left behind in Malta hospital on the outward voyage. Theirs has been a chequered existence since that time;

now one ship, now another, until up to this time they can reckon up eight such shifts.

December 4th.—Whilst coaling at Amoy an accident happened, which has resulted in the death of another of our poor fellows, George Allen, an ordinary seaman. Whilst he and a companion were on a visit to a Chinese gunboat in the harbour, and both, it is to be feared, under the influence of liquor, Allen slipped as he was mounting the side, fell overboard, and was not seen afterward. Strangely enough, the man who was with him had not the slightest idea of the occurrence, and it was not until the captain of the Chinaman came on board the following morning and reported the circumstance, that we became aware that we had lost a shipmate. Before sailing we were joined by the " Egeria," and as it was the admiral's intention to visit Swatow we called in at Hope bay to allow him to turn over to the " Egeria " for that purpose. We arrived in Hong Kong on December 15th.

And now, dear reader, I have accomplished the round of our station, and have got through, I trust, to your satisfaction, the most difficult part of this narrative, viz. : the descriptive. Henceforward, to avoid tiring and useless repetition I shall refer you to the appendix for ports visited, only taking up for narrative purposes, such events in our subsequent history as I shall deem of major importance. If I do not adopt some such plan as this my book will far exceed its intended limits.

December 25th.—If we may believe the old saw, there are some things which have the misfortune to suffer by comparison. Accepting this as fact, the Christmas of last year must hide its diminished head before its present anniversary. We were determined on making our lower deck as home-like as possible, to deceive ourselves—pleasant fiction!—into the belief that there were not 120 degrees of longitude between us and our friends. The admiral behaved like a brick, by contributing largely to the good cheer. The mess-deck just showed how tastefully sailors can do things in the way of "get ups" when left to their own devices and resources. As Christmas, 1880, was by far the jolliest Christmas day we have spent during our sojourn in China, I will not anticipate by describing the present, but will reserve for a subsequent page the pleasure of telling you all about it.

CHAPTER XIII.

*"And there on reef we come to grief,
Which has often occurred to we."*

IN WHICH WE ATTEMPT AN OVERLAND ROUTE, WITH THE RESULT OF THE TRIAL.

HAIL, all hail, to the glad new year! What though there be no crisp seasonable snow, no exhilarating frost, no cosy chimney nooks, or no ladies muffs and comfortable ulsters? Let us joy at 'his birth all the same, for does he not mark another year nearer the end? —of the commission I mean.

And now to work. At the annual inspection of our heavy guns it was found that three at least were so defective in the bore that it was necessary to condemn them, and replace them by new ones. This entailed a terrible amount of labour on our men. Hatchways had to be torn to pieces, and yards rigged with most ponderous blocks, and purchases for the safe transhipment of these iron playthings. Whatever may be urged against, there is this to be said in favour of such heavy and unusal evolutions, that observant men gain largely in practical experience and an extended acquaintance with the "might be's" of their profession. Fortunately, in one sense, but few commissions afford such unwelcome opportunities as ours, for it has been one of accidental, rather than of meditated experiment.

In the midst of dismal rainy weather the business of refitting had to be pushed forward, previous to our going in dock; then coaling and painting—in our ship separate work—and provisioning, swallowed up the greater part of the month of January.

February 11th.—To-day the "Tyne" arrived from England. To the expatiated seaman the arrival of a troopship has a greater interest than have ordinary arrivals; for has she not scarce two months since, perhaps, looked on the very scenes we so long to behold? She is thus a link between us and home. Then there is also the additional interest of seeing fresh faces, whilst to the more fortunate who are about to leave us she is the absorbing topic. She remained only eight days. On the occasion of her departure we were allowed to cheer—a wonderful concession; at the same time we were given clearly to understand that we were to accept it in the light of a great privilege; and that there should be no mistake on this point, the commander conducted the arrangements with the order "Three cheers for H.M.S. 'Tyne,' homeward bound;" "And no extras," added somebody in parenthesis.

* * * * *

And now came April 15th, not so rapidly as would appear from the above sketch; but it came, and with it the commencement of a second voyage to the northward.

In the interval between the sailing of the "Tyne" and

our departure we were not idle. We had gone outside twice—once at target practice and once on steam tactics. The "Armide," French flag-ship, had left for Europe, and her relief, the "Thémis," had arrived on the station, losing several sheets of copper off her starboard bow on the passage up from Singapore.

It is curious to observe the different customs of foreign sailors when sailing, homeward bound. The French, for instance, rig up a dummy man and trice him up to the main top, where he is made to oscillate with a pendulum movement until he gains sufficient impetus to clear the side, when he is let go overboard amidst the cheering of the men. The Russians man yards, white caps in hand, which, after waving in the air to make their cheering more energetic, they fling into the sea.

But to return to April 15th.—We had but cleared Hong Kong when we sighted the "Charybdis," with the long pennant flying. Fortunate fellows! how long, I wonder, before we shall be similarly decorated? I write this almost three years afterwards, and still the question remains unanswered.

On the way we put in to White Dogs, in expectation of finding the "Vigilant" with our mail. The mails latterly have been very erratic in their arrivals, due to a change in the postal system at home. Henceforth there is to be no penny mail—a fact which, seemingly, our friends have not yet grasped; hence it is no uncommon thing to go weeks without letters, and then suddenly to find oneself inundated with—say six or eight *billets deux*.

The "Vigilant" was only a few hours behind us; and after giving us our mail she left for Foo-chow, with the admiral and captain on board.

That night we rode out a very stiff gale. The seas were so heavy that all ports had to be barred in, and even then, such was the violence of the storm that water was occasionally shipped through the upper battery ports. From the manner in which the cable "surged" and bumbed, it was deemed expedient to let go a second anchor, and to get up steam; for in the event of the wind chopping around —nothing more likely—we should be on a dead lee shore, and our only alternative to slip and go to sea. Still the gale increased, and still the one anchor and cable held. How the wind did howl and screech through our cordage! This lasted for over two days. On the third day the "Moorhen" came down from Foo-chow with our captain; and as their was still a big lump of a sea on, she capered about in the lively manner peculiar to gun vessels.

April 21st.—We rounded the Shun-tung promontory in a thick fog, groped our way towards Chefoo in the same hazy atmosphere, and picked up our anchorage in nearly the same spot as last year, glad enough to get in anywhere out of such dangerous weather.

The cutter's crew of the "Pegasus," a day or two after our arrival, reminded us of a challenge they had previously thrown out, to pull any boat of similar size in our ship for forty-five dollars. Accordingly, one fine afternoon when the sea was as smooth as a pond, and on the occasion of a dance given by our officers, the contest came off. Contrary to the expectations of most, our boat beat almost without an effort. That same evening the "Lily's," with more pluck than discretion, tossed their oars under our bows. Well, like a great good-tempered Newfoundland dog, we can stand a deal of snapping at from insignificant puppies, but when at length their attacks begin to get acrimonious, we rise, and shake our shaggy coat; and in salt water language "*go*" for the torments. Thus we "*went*" for the "Lily's," beat them, and pocketed thirty-six dollars more.

On the arrival of the admiral a court-martial was held on a marine, of the "Mosquito," for insubordination. I mention this because of the extreme sentence of the court—twenty-five lashes with the "cat." The admiral, though, came to the rescue, and with mercy seasoned justice, for he refused to sign the warrant for the punishment.

We left Chefoo for Japan, calling in at the Golo islands —a group about 90 miles from Nagasaki—on the way. 'Twas a lovely spot, and recent rains had made nature look all the fairer for her ablutions. The gentle breeze wafted off such a delightful fragrance of pine, fir, hay, and flowers, so welcome after China's reeking smells. Slowly, and with caution, we wended our way up an intricate channel, meandering amongst the hills in a most striking and artistic manner, until further progress was barred, by the shores of a tiny bay, with a town at its head. We found ourselves so perfectly land-locked that everybody was wondering how we got in. Around us high volcanic hills, and under us,—not a volcano—but, between twenty and thirty fathoms of water. We could not anchor here, that was evident, so we set the spanker, slued about, and made tracks as rapidly as we could before the darkness should set in. Next morning we were at Nagasaki.

Early on the morning of the 29th of May we sailed for the eastward, by way of the Inland Seas. We turned slightly out of our course to call at Yobuko, a real bit of Japan, lovely and enchanting. We were objects of absorbing interest to the simple islanders. They wore very primitive and airy garments, some even none at all. They are not much like, in fact very unlike, a community of Japanese; for cleanliness amongst them is an " unknown quantity;" and their dwellings remind me very forcibly of the squalid dens in Chinese native towns. The people, though, were hospitable and kind to a degree, and highly glad to see us, offering us of their little saké and tea— nor would they take money, or accept any payment, though we pressed it upon them. At first they were shy, following us about in curious, respectful, distant crowds; but seeing we treated their chubby little children kindly they soon made friends with us.

We reached Kobé in due course where nothing of moment took place, if we except a gale of wind which compelled our liberty-men—*much against their will*, of course—to remain on shore all night. " Well ' *'tis* an ill wind that blows *nobody* good,' is it not ? "

July 2nd.—We are at Yokohama, and are a-taut; for to-day some members of the Japanese imperial family are to visit us. At noon they arrived amidst salvoes of artillery from the shore and from the Japanese men-of-war. The party consisted of prince Arisugawa's father and sister, her maids of honor, and two admirals. The princess was of course the " lion "—excuse the gender— of the party. But how lost, how utterly bewildered, she looked in reaching our quarter-deck! like little Alice in wonderland. I hear it is the first time she has ever been afloat. Her style of dress is different to anything we have yet seen in this country. A red silk skirt clothed her lower limbs, whilst a transparent gauzy purple tunic, figured with the imperial emblem, fell from her shoulders to the ground. But her hair was what drew most of our attention, for it was the most remarkable piece of head architecture possible. How shall I describe it? Imagine a frying-pan inverted, its inner rim resting on the crown of the head, and the handle depending down the back, and you will have a correct, though a homely idea, of the fashion of her hair. Each individual hair seemed as if picked out from it fellows, stiffened by some process until it appeared like a wire bent into shape; gathered in and tied a little below the nape of the neck, and from thence downward traced into a queue. Hers was the ideal type of Japanese feature, so rarely seen amongst the common people, and considered so unlovely by Europeans. A long face, narrow straight nose, almond eyes, very obliquely set in the head, and a mouth so tiny, so thin the upper lip, that it looks more like a scarlet button than anything designed for kissing.

She was childishly pleased at everything she saw whilst accompanying the admiral around the decks, twitching at his arm incessantly that she might indulge her curiosity as to hatchways, stoke-hole gratings, and so on; clapping her hands continually in the exuberance of her joy.

The "Modeste" accompanied us in our trip to the north on this occasion.

A few days out we called in at Kamaishi, in the neighbourhood of which are the imperial copper mines and smelting works. The people here lack the rosiness and freshness of face of the Japanese, and have a dowdy, sickly look, due, I suppose, to the unhealthy exhalations from the copper.

Instead of calling in at Hakodadi we continued on along the eastern coast of Yezo until we reached Endermo harbour, sentinelled at its entrance by a grim vomiting volcano which, in addition to its charred and fire-scored crater, has innumerable other little outlets in its sides, giving out jets of steam and sulphurous smoke until the very air is loaded with the oppressive vapour.

At the anchorage we saw the " Pegasus."

Here we are then ! in the country of Miss Bird's Aïnos, a people whom she describes as the most gentle and docile in the world. We had ample opportunity of making their acquaintance, for during our stay the decks were daily thronged with them. In these men the advocates of Darwinism might well behold the missing link. From head to heel they are covered with thick shaggy unkempt masses of hair ; that on their heads and faces hanging down in wild elfish locks. They wear but scant raiment, a sort of over-all, which does not pretend to the use of even the most primitive covering. It is of the men I speak. Strangely enough, though, they all have their ears pierced, metal ornaments are not worn by any, but, instead, they have a thin strip of scarlet cloth, just simply placed through the hole. The women are strange looking creatures. Their garments are modest enough, far more so even than those of their southern sisters with whom, by the way, they have nothing in common, save their sex, Can it be that this is the primitive Japanese race—that the more enlightened people of Niphon trace their origin to such a degraded source? I should be inclined to say no, if I did not remember that history furnishes us with so many parallel cases of similar degraded origin—our own for example.

Well built, but oh! so ugly these women; and, as if nature had not done enough for them in this particular, they render their faces still more repulsive looking by tattooing the lips on the outside to the depth of an inch all around, elongating the mark at the corners. This, of course, does not tend to lessen the apparent size of an aperture, already suggestive of a main hatchway. This unhandsome, open, flat countenance, is also further decorated with bands of blue on the forehead. The females wear large rings of iron—some few of silver—in their ears.

Now, though of course I don't pretend to the faithfulness of portraiture, nor to the accuracy of observation of the travelled lady I have before quoted, yet I must add that my estimate of this people, in my own small way, is antagonistic to hers. To me they are only a very little removed from savages. Their women seem to be in abject slavery to the men, and are treated by them in the most shameful manner. An instance, which came under my own observation, will perhaps shew this. Whilst on shore fishing, I had wandered away from the main party to where I saw a native engaged at work on an upturned canoe. Up the beach was his hut—I have seen many a stye a king to it—and in the doorway his—wife must I call her? Curious I suppose like all her sex she came down the strand to get a look at the white-skinned, light-haired stranger, and was rewarded for temerity in a most summary manner. The man, at first, seemed to expostulate with her, and so far as I could judge, ordered her back to her domicile; but as the lady did not seem prompt to obey the mandate, he further emphasised his meaning and accelerated her movements by flinging a billet of wood at her with all the irresponsible and unrestrained force of a savage nature. In the face of this can I agree with Miss Bird? My first feeling was one of indignation and an angry twitching of my ten digits to form themselves into bunches of fives, but on second thoughts, seeing that the poor woman took the chastisement as a matter of course, and that she was seemingly used to such like gentle reminders, my indignation cooled down to matter of fact surprise.

This place is the exile home of one of the banished daïmios I spoke of in a former chapter.

From Endermo we retraced ours steps to Hakodadi, where, during a short stay, we had some amusement in the shape of messes pulling for bags of "spuds" (the potatoe of the non-sailor world) and other comestibles.

July 30th.—The date of the most important event of the commission. Referring to my "journal" I find recorded below this date that word of terrible import, "*stranded.*" Yea, truly are we. And this is how it all came about. We had sailed from Hakodadi with a fair wind, through the strait of Sangar and out into the sea of Japan, shaped our course for Aniwa bay, in Sagalien, with —except that the atmosphere was rather hazy—every prospect of a fair and quick passage.

Off the south western corner of Yezo, and about ninety

miles from Hakodadi, lies the small island of O'Kosiri, in the track of vessels going north. By morning we had reached its neighbourhood—it could be seen in fact—when suddenly a thick fog enveloped it, us, and the surrounding sea. We were to have gone outside the island, though the inner passage is navigable, still, to avoid any possibility of an accident, it was deemed best to go to seaward of it. At 4 a.m., whilst steaming at six knots, the look out man reported land dead ahead. The officer of the watch, seemingly pretty confident as to his whereabouts, altered course a point or so, and kept on at the same speed. An hour passed, the fog had settled thicker than ever. At ten minutes past two bells in the morning, without any warning—the lead even shewing deep soundings—a crashing, grating sound was heard, accompanied by a distinct trembling vibration, proceeding, apparently, from under the ship's bottom. Even then, no one dreamed we were ashore; such a sound, such a sensation, might have been produced by running over a junk. At this moment the leadsman got a throw of the lead, and "*a quarter less four,*" indicated only too plainly the origin of the sounds.

With his usual promptness—as if running ashore was a matter of ordinary evolution—our captain at once gave orders for engines to be reversed, for boats to be hoisted out, and anchors placed away, where they would be of most use; at the same time directions were given to have the steam launch coaled and provisioned to go back to Hakodadi for assistance. On soundings being taken along the starboard side plenty of water was obtained; it was only on her port bottom that the ship had grounded. Efforts were made to roll her off, all hands rushing from one side of the deck to the other, but without result. Through the crystal clear water, and in the deep shadow of the ship, the nature of the bottom could be clearly seen—coral rocks and yellow sand. Fortunately the sea was a flat calm, or it must have fared ill indeed with us.

At ordinary times the sailor prefers plenty of sea room, and the further he is from land the safer he feels; but when one's ship has suddenly converted "*mare*" into "*terram*" with, may be, a hole in her to boot, then indeed the proximity to some friendly shore is his first consideration.

The lifting fog revealed to us our whereabouts; within a hundred yards of us the surf washed edges of a reef, and before us the low shores and high hills of O'Kosiri.

The unusual sight of a large ship so near their island soon brought the natives off in their queer canoes. By means of our interpreter we learn that the people had never seen a man-of-war before; that there was no rise and fall of tide there; and much more about the ways and means available for opening up communications with Hakodadi.

Meanwhile shot and shell were got out and sent on shore, and coals pitched overboard, because no lighters were obtainable at this stage in the proceedings. The divers having gone down reported the ship aground in three distinct places, aft, amidships under the batteries, and forward. Thus ended the first day. With the morrow a swell set in from seaward, which caused us to bump heavily, though it did not alter our position. On this day the expected assistance arrived from Hakodadi. Close on each other's heels the following ships bore down upon us :—the "Modeste," with lighters in tow, the "Kerguelen," "Champlain," and "Thémis," Frenchmen, the latter the admiral's ship; and the Russian corvette "Naezdnik," with the admiral's flag at the mizen.

These five ships at once anchored in the best positions consistent with their own safety to help us; the "Kerguelen" a little on our starboard quarter, and the "Champlain" right astern with our steel hawsers on board and two anchors down.

With the second night came a chapter of accidents.

At sunset a rolling sea again set in, heavier than that of the morning. The swell and the weight of our hawsers acting on the necessarily short cables of the "Champlain," caused that vessel to drag and take the ground on our port quarter. In her attempts to extricate herself, our steel hawser got foul of her propeller and wound itself around it in such a confused mass, that the vessel's machinery became practically useless. Thus, side by side, the two companions in distress kept the watches of that night. But this was not all; the "Modeste" coming to the rescue of the "Champlain," ran into the "Kerguelen," but fortunately without any serious result.

Sunday, August 1st.—At daylight the "Modeste" succeeded in towing the "Champlain" out of her perilous position. As she did so a large piece of the Frenchman's false keel floated to the surface, whilst she was found to be making two and a half tons of water per hour. A turn of her propeller the other way caused the now useless hawser to fall off. When recovered by the divers, this mass of steel wire was a gordian knot of utter confusion.

The swell of last night, though it did our ship and the "Champlain" some harm, rendered us at least one service, by causing a higher influx of water than usual, which resulted in lifting us off our pinnacled and dangerous resting place into deep soundings again. And now it was discovered that we too were taking in water in one of our compartments which, however, thanks to our double bottom system, we were enabled to confine to the one space.

As we passed slowly by the anchored ships, cheer after cheer rent the still air, whilst the bands played our national anthem. An analysis of the sounds of this multitudinous chorus of men's voices, was a very interesting, though not a difficult matter. The sweet cadence of the Frenchmen's low cheer was clearly a distinct sound from the Russian's ursine growl; whilst the Englishmen's "hip, hip, hurrah!" if not so musical as the first, nor as bearish as the second, was a more honest sound than either.

On the following evening, after having bundled all our stores on board, we put back to Hakodadi for coal and to allow the admiral to turn over to the "Modeste."

August 6th.—Off for Hong Kong by the Japan sea passage, touching at Nagasaki for coal, and hence on to Amoy against a south-west monsoon, and into the scorching heat of the southern summer. A few hours at Amoy sufficed us to take in enough coal for the short distance to Hong Kong, where we had the satisfaction of finding ourselves, without mishap, on August 18th. Almost immediately the hands were sent on board the "Victor Emmanuel," whilst the ship was undergoing repairs at Aberdeen.

Whilst resting on the chocks in the dock the extent of the damage sustained by us was plainly visible; and, when we come to consider, that fourteen plates had to be removed and replaced by new ones, and this too in the immediate neighbourhood of the keel, the wonder is that Chinamen accomplished the cumbrous work satisfactorily.

September 20th.—Exactly one month ago to-day the ship was docked—to-day she came out; what do you think of that for expedition? On floating it was found that a slight damage to the Kingston valve had been overlooked, and as the ship was still making water, it was thought a second docking would be necessary. Fortunately our very effective diving staff were able to repair it without the bother and additional expense of being shored up again.

September 22nd.—A red-letter day. Why? Oh, only because—"tell it not in Gath"—the captain "*spliced the main brace!*" Yea, yea, verily! The fact was, his ship had been got ready for sea in *two days*; hence the *splicing*.

September 23rd.—We were to have gone to sea to-day, but "*l'homme propose.*" Rumours of an approaching atmospheric disturbance had been telegraphed from Manilla, within the previous forty-eight hours. Other usual and confirmatory indications were also observed; the presence of an unusual number of jelly-fish in the harbour till the sea stank with them; the lurid appearance of the sunset sky, as if the heavens were bathed in blood; the arrival of hundreds of junks from seaward seeking shelter: all these signs summed up were considered satisfactory reasons for preparing for a typhoon—than which, I suppose, no wind is more violent and destructive. It is said that persons who have never witnessed the sublime and terrible spectacle can scarcely realize, even from the most graphic descriptions of eye witnesses, what a typhoon really means. A Chinaman informed me that the last typhoon destroyed not less than 18,000 persons in this neighbourhood alone—not a large number when we bear in mind the enormous floating populations in Chinese towns. All the day the air was ominous of a coming something. At noon I asked a Chinaman when it might be expected. His answer shewed me how even this mighty destroyer is guided by a far mightier hand—"Suppose he no' com now, he com by'm by, nine clock." Well, "he" did not come now; but at 9 p.m.—and almost simultaneous with the firing of the gun—it came on to blow; but, mercifully, not a typhoon, only the spent violence of one. Even this necessitated the letting go a second anchor and the steaming head on to it, for upwards of five hours.

With the morning the gale had considerably abated, and as the barometer was on the rise, and the captain impatient to clear out, we put to sea. But clearly the weather was in a very unsettled state, and outside Amoy the glass again went down with a rising head sea. That we might put into Amoy for shelter, all the furnaces were called into requisition; so we lashed into and almost buried ourselves in seas rearing themselves up a-head of us like walls of solid glass. We brought up in the outer harbour just as the shades of night and the roar of the coming storm gathered around us. That night the wind and sea played fast and furious with our ship; again we had escaped a typhoon—it was subsequently ascertained that one did actually visit the adjacent coasts and sea; but, as this wind travels in a circle of many miles diameter, with its greatest force distributed near its circumference, its centre only passed over Amoy. On steaming seaward the next morning desolation, destruction, and wreck were everywhere manifest.

In due course we reached Nagasaki. In the bay was the Russian iron-clad, "Minin," a ship—if all we hear about her be true—capable of blowing the "Iron Duke" sky-high. She is, however, inferior to us in many desirable qualities, particularly in the essential one of being able to keep the sea, and fight her guns in all weathers. The "Comus," one of our handsome steel corvettes, was also here.

The hard steaming from Nagasaki, against exceptionally heavy winds, had pretty well cleared us out of coal, and, as there was not enough in store here to supply us with, we were ordered off to Kobé to fill up.

On our return, and just as we had cleared the strait of Liminoseki, we fell in with what sailors term nasty weather. The ship behaved so saucily that a seaman, Alexander Mann, whilst engaged lashing the anchor was washed completely overboard and borne away astern. Daniel Mutch, the captain of his top—a petty-officer who has already been instrumental in saving life at sea—observing the accident, at once rushed aft to the stern, plunged boldly into the turbulent waves and succeeded in rescuing his topmate. It is satisfactory to be able to state that the captain recognised Mutch's bravery by applying for the Humane Society's Medal, which honorable decoration was received shortly afterwards.

Next day an event of a similar nature, but unfortunately with a sadder termination, took place. In setting the starboard stunsail, John Irish, A.B., lost his hold of the scarping on the starboard fore-and-aft bridge, through the wood treacherously giving away with his weight, and, being unable to swim, the poor fellow soon sank exhausted, just as Joseph Summers had arrived on the spot. Irish had but lately come into a legecy from some of his friends at home.

Early in December we left Nagasaki for Hong Kong, touching at the Rugged Isles, on the opposite Chinese coast, on the passage. We spent about as uncomfortable a week in this delicious retreat as can be well conceived; our appetites sharpened to a keen edge by a north China winter—a week never to be forgotten. Opportunely the admiral came in at the expiration of time and terminated our miseries by ordering us to proceed.

December 20th.—To-day, and on the two subsequent days, the "one gun salute" at eight bells from the "Victor Emanuel" announced that somebody's fate was to be sealed. Three of our officers—the captain, staff-commander, and Lieutenant Clarke—are to be tried on a charge, preferred by the admiral, of negligently stranding Her Majesty's Ship "Iron Duke." Much interest naturally centred around this trial; the reporters from the local papers exerting themselves to the utmost for information on such an engrossing topic. On the third day the sentence of the court was announced :—the captain and Mr. Clarke to be reprimanded, and the staff-commander to be severely so.

December 25th.—To fulfil a promise of twelve months'

standing, from the 20th to the 25th discipline was relaxed that we might prepare for our one festival; and as the admiral had again rendered us pecuniary help, and as this would be his last Christmas with us we were determined on making it a success. Meanwhile, whilst the decorations are pushing ahead, I must pause to notice the naval regatta of the 23rd, and especially the race which came about between our cutter and a similar boat of the "Lily," which it will be remembered we beat at Chefoo recently; but so confident were the "Lily's" that our victory on that occasion was the result of a "fluke," that they challenged us again to pull for sixty dollars. The race was conclusive to the "Lily's," and they handed over the "Mexicans" with the best grace a small ship's company can be supposed to exhibit—on the eve of Christmas, too.

An interesting feature in the regatta, and one which caused no end of fun, was the get-up of the copper punts. These naval abortions are, for the nonce, handed over to the funny fellows on board, who proceed to elect a "captain," and appoint themselves to the various offices connected with the proper management of their craft. With great rapidity and no little skill these punts are metamorphosed into brigs, full-rigged ships, paddle-wheeled steamers, and ram-bowed ironclads. The "captain's" get-up is the most gorgeous and elaborate thing possible—a profusion of gold lace, a monster cocked hat suitable for the top of the great pyramid, and a tremendous speaking trumpet whose bore would do very well for a tunnel. His crew generally attire themselves in the fantastic dress of niggers. Just as the proceedings for the day were about to begin, a pigmy paddler was

M

observed bearing down on the flag-ship—her puffing funnel and foaming bows betraying no mean steam power. On closing she was made out to be one of the punt fleet come to pay a visit to the admiral. As she lay to she ran the St. George's Cross up to the main, and saluted it with seventeen guns (wooden ones), out of compliment to Admiral Coote, who shortly receives his promotion. She next asked permission (by signal) to part company, a request the admiral answered by hoisting the affirmative. It was indeed real fun.

By the 24th our lower deck looked a veritable fairy bower, but essentially English—a character which the arrival of the "Thèmis," on Christmas eve, modified somewhat. With characteristic good feeling and with, perhaps, a spice of national vanity, we determined on asking the Frenchmen to dine with us on the morrow— first, because having just come in from sea they would be unable to prepare for themselves; and, secondly, that we might shew them how Englishmen observe Christmas day. Our invitation asked that three hundred men might be allowed to come, but half that number only could be spared.

It now became necessary to make our surroundings as international as possible, and as, happily, the French flag does not demand any very great skill in its formation, we soon had the tri-color stuck up everywhere; whilst in the most conspicuous positions French mottoes shewed out from the greenery. The wording of these latter was a tremendous effort, so limited was our knowledge of our nearest neighbour's tongue. Just to quote a few:—surrounding every pudding a scroll with "Bien venue

'Thèmis'" painted on it; in the mess shelves, "Vive la France;" whilst, occupying a commanding place, the following long yarn—"Servons nous votre reine mais honneur à la republique français," shone out in great gilt letters. Then, too, there were plenty of legends in English; and noticing these, one would be surprised at the wit, no less than at the talent, exhibited in their execution. For example, here is a sailor depicted with a most lugubrious and "I-wish-I-might-get-it" expression on his rather florid face, looking into an empty grog-tub; and that there may be no ambiguity about the matter, the word *empty* is printed on the tub, and attached to his mouth a balloon-shaped sack containing the following visible speech—"Three years on the 'Alert' but no 'Discovery.'" A second tar is represented holding a stranded rope up to his captain, whilst he naïvely remarks, "It wants splicing, sir." There were also several mottoes specially designed as compliments to the admiral.

At noon on Christmas day we awaited on the quarter deck the arrival of our guests, who, as soon as they came inboard were ushered below and placed in the posts of honor at the tables. After the admiral, captain, and officers had made the round of the decks, preceded by the band playing the immortal strains of "The roast beef of Old England," the shrill whistles piped "fall-to."

And now might have been witnessed a laughable scene, men rushing and hurrying about here, there, and everywhere, exclaiming "Have you seen our Frenchmen?" or "I've lost a Frenchman," and so on. But at length the lost were found, and were, ere long, contemplating the formidable heap of indigestible stuff set before them.

Such mountains of pudding, goose, ham, mutton, beef, and pickles—all packed on one plate—I suppose it rarely falls to the lot of the more polished Frenchman to behold. Well might they look aghast at the miracle required of them. It is the proverbial hospitality of the Englishman, enacted over again, which always imagines its guest starving. Considering that not one word of the other's language was understood on either side, a very kindly feeling sprang up between us during the afternoon, and the time of departure arrived all too soon. After the tea, which was to all intents and purposes a repetition of the mid-day meal, the Frenchmen's boats came alongside, the crews invited inboard and loaded with the débris of the feast. When at length they left us, the Frenchmen all stood up in their boats, whilst we lined our bridges and spar deck, and a succession of deafening cheers brought the happy day to a close—cheers which most of the ships in port took up as the boats passed their bows. So ended Christmas, 1880.

CHAPTER XIV.

"Each earing to its cringle first they bend—
The reef-band then along the yard extend;
The circling earings round th' extremes entwin'd,
By outer and by inner turns they bind;
The reeflines next from hand to hand received,
Through eyelet-holes and roban legs were reeved;
The folding reefs in plaits unrolled they lay,
Extend the worming lines and ends belay."

THE NEW REGIME.—SOMETHING ABOUT SAIGON.—THE FIRST CRUISE OF THE CHINA SQUADRON.—AN ALARM OF FIRE!—ARRIVAL OF THE "FLYING" SQUADRON.

SUNDAY, January 2nd.—For some time past we have been exercised to know how we could best signify to the admiral our appreciation of his many kindnesses to us during the time we have served under him. His approaching promotion gave us the desired opportunity, and it was decided that the most fitting present would be a silk flag of the largest size, to be hoisted at the main on that auspicious occasion. With this end in view we had purchased some 130 yards of silk at Nagasaki, which had been made up on board so quietly that few even of those most interested in it knew of its progress.

To day he was to hoist his flag as full admiral for the first time; and on this morning a deputation of the ship's company awaited on him in his cabin to make the presentation. The captain, in a few suitable words, having introduced the representatives, and the admiral having responded to their presentation address in simple, unaffected, heartfelt language, the flag was soon fluttering in lazy folds aloft, to be saluted at "eight bells" by the shore battery and foreign men-of-war in harbour. A most innocent thing that flag, and scarcely could we conceive that it was destined to become the occasion of newspaper paragraphs, parliamentary questionings, admiralty minutes, and that sort of thing, but it was so to be. By one of the regulations of the service no officer may receive presents or testimonials from his men—hence the correspondence. It is, however, satisfactory to know that in the present instance the admiralty allowed the admiral to retain our flag.

January 7th.—To-day's mail proved a complete hoax. By it we were speedily to be relieved—so said all our private letters, so corroborated the officers, and even the admiral seemed to give a certain amount of credence to the rumour. But need I say it was a chimera. The papers are to blame for all this; for they stated that Admiral Willes had inspected the "Swiftsure" and had found her in every way fit for his flag-ship. This was all true; but what wasn't, was—that she is to come out to relieve us.

February 16th.—A month since—and if anyone had asked us where we should be bound when next we slipped from the buoy, we should have answered with a joyful "*homeward!*" To-day we know better. We are speeding Singapore-ward, it is true, but not to meet our relief. The voyage into those torrid seas was not momentous, and a week afterwards we lay alongside the coaling jetty before spoken of.

And now we became aware that quite an unexpected and perhaps in some respects—judging from after experience—not altogether a welcome change was about to be made in our executive. The admiral, of course, leaves under any circumstances; but, further, the captain, commander, and staff-commander were to be superseded, their reliefs being already on the passage out. In addition, the chaplain and Mr. Clarke were to leave, though at their own request.

By the mail of the 26th the first instalment of our fresh officers arrived. These were the admiral, G. O. Willes, of Devonport dockyard celebrity and traditionally known to us; the commander, nephew to the admiral; and the flag lieutenant.

January 28th.—So quietly, that the majority of us scarce knew of it, the admiral left to-day for England, and with him the good wishes of everybody on the lower deck. With the hauling down of the flag at the main, and its re-hoisting at the fore, a new departure in the conduct of the fleet on the China station was inaugurated. Henceforth a season of activity, seasoned with salt junk, is to be the order of the day.

After a short cruise with the squadron in Singapore waters, during which period the "Tyne" arrived with our new captain, and having bid good-bye to Captain Cleveland, we stood away for Hong Kong, encountering such heavy weather on the passage that we were compelled to put into Saigon for coal.

The anchorage to seaward of Saigon—which town is the French capital of Gambodin, part of the kingdom of Anam, and situated some miles up the river Dong-nai—is Cape St. James, where we brought up until the tide should suit for the river passage. In the first watch we commenced to go up the river by the light of a brilliant moon, which, however, did not allow us to judge of the beauties of what is really a beautiful river. By the following morning we had arrived off the town; and what a surprise it was to see a popular European town in such a situation, well laid out, clean, and—well, thoroughly French. The river here is so narrow, and yet of so even a depth, that, in turning, our dolphin striker was buried in the foliage on the one bank and our stern almost touching the opposite one. The town is seemingly built on a well-drained swamp or marsh, and consequently lies very low, in fact, from our topgallant forecastle we could command a pretty general view of the whole of it. Ashore the place is just as pretty as it looks from the ship. It is almost a miniature of Paris. A great cathedral, Notre Dame—an exact model of that on the island in the Seine; a palace for the governor, which might well accommodate an emperor; streets with Parisian names; boulevards and champs, all bearing the well-known nomenclature of the gay capital; cafés, hotels, all remind one of the Paris of Dumas' charming novels. It is the boulevards, streets, and promenades, planted with trees, which make Saigon so beautiful, so cool, and so refreshing towards the evening even in a temperature where to live is a punishment. It is not until sunset that we see anything of the French population,—then, indeed, the cafés and restaurants are in full swing, and gay with music and laughter. These places of refreshment are generally *al fresco* ; and as each tiny pure white marble table is presided over by pretty wholesome-looking French girls and matrons, we must have less impressionable hearts than sailors are known to possess if we can pass so much mischief by unnoticed, so courteous as these demoiselles are too.

The native populaton is Anamese, a race something like the Chinese in feature, but differing from them slightly in dress. They do not shave the head, but gather all their hair into a knot at the top, which—in the case of the females—they decorate with rolls of brilliantly colored silks, generally scarlet or emerald green. The dress of the ladies is far more graceful than that of their " celestial " sisters, for though they wear the indispensable trousers, yet that masculine garment is hid by a long sack-like robe, something after the style of a priest's toga, of—in nearly every case—emerald-green silk, a color which seems to harmonise well with their complexion. The men wear a similar garment of black silk.

Their walk is peculiar. They go barefoot, and strut, rather than walk, without bending the knee, with chest and stomach pompously projected. From this gait results a certain balancing of the body and a movement to the hips, which gives to the women a bold, and to the men a pretentious air. Most of the women hide their faces when a stranger heaves in sight; but it must not be supposed from this that they are either modest or retiring, on the contrary, for young girls and women yield their persons indiscriminately to men until they are married: before that they are at liberty to do as they please, and do not, in consequence, lose the respect of their fellows. In fact, I am given to understand, most strangers find the advances of the fair sex rather embarrassing.

At the landing place, and thronging the fine bronze statute of Admiral Genouilly, the hero of Saigon, an immense crowd had gathered to witness the embarkation of the governor, on a visit to our admiral. His barge is a splendidly got up affair. A large boat of native build, painted and gilded till one could scarcely look on it, and rowed by fourteen French seamen standing, clothed in spotless white, with broad crimson sashes around their waists. This equipage had such a holiday look about it, that one of our fellows irreverently asked if "Sanger's circus was coming!"

Only a day at Saigon, and off again. Instead of shaping course direct for Hong Kong we hugged the coast of Cochin China, thinking thus to cheat the monsoon. In this we were mistaken, for the wind and sea proved so strong that lower yards and topmasts had to be struck. Thus it was not until the 25th, and after hard steaming, that we reached Hong Kong.

April 16th.—To-day, William Edwards, second captain of the main top, died in hospital of a complication of debilitating complaints.

April 21st.—Started on our yearly trip. Between Hong Kong and Amoy we encountered a series of baffling fogs, compelling us to anchor for days at a stretch. One clear day the "Lapwing" passed, bound for Hong Kong. She had recently been in collision with a Chinese merchant steamer, and inflicted such telling damage on the latter that now her bones lie rotting at the bottom of the Formosa channel.

At Amoy we found the first division of the cruising squadron at anchor, under the command of Captain East, of the "Comus." From Hong Kong here they had been under the convoy of the admiral, who had, to use an expression of one of the interested, given them a thorough "shaking up," especially in the night watches.

Before sailing the "kit" of our late deceased shipmate was disposed of at a public auction, and realised the sum of £25. This, together with a general subscription, allowed us to send the comfortable sum of £100 to his widow. It is at these sales that one sees the sailor come out in—what shall I say, a new character? Well, in a way, yes; for he certainly exhibits a carefulness of thought and an enlargement of the organ of feeling, for which the world would scarce give him credit perhaps. I have often thought it the most beautiful trait in an otherwise rough and crude nature. Let it but be known that a poor woman is left helpless to struggle through a hard and selfish world, may-be children to add to her difficulties, then you shall see that the sailor's heart is in the right place; then all private animosity against the deceased is swallowed up in the "charity which is kind." The ancient Romans were not more eager to obtain a memento of dead Cæsar than they for some article of the deceased's clothing; not so much for the sake of the thing itself, but simply that, by the purchase of it, they may exercise their generosity, by giving for it, perhaps, four times its value.

We have orders to cruise to Chefoo *under sail.* Fancy an iron-clad making a passage under canvas! With the "Iron Duke's" usual luck we encountered either boisterous head winds or flat calms all the way, compelling us to reef our canvas or to endure the tantalizing and provoking agony of witnessing our sails hang in picturesque, but useless, festoons up and down the masts.

For ten days we scarce saw the sun; for ten days the sextants lay idle. When at length the sun did condescend to slash the sky with his hopeful beams, we found we had made the satisfactory average of *ten miles* a day. Our potatoes, too,—that self-provided esculent upon which sailors depend so much, and without which the admiralty allowance assumes such skeleton proportions—now began to fail us. As it was useless to attempt to reach Chefoo under sail alone, steam was got up, and we managed to make the harbour on June 6th.

Here again we picked up the squadron and the admiral, the former of whom had been lying idle for fourteen days, eating of the fat of the land, whilst we, like certain ruminants, have been consuming our own fat, for want of more natural food.

On the 11th, the squadron departed for evolutions in the gulf of Ne-chili, outside, the admiral accompanying to put them through a little practice.

Whilst at Chefoo, this time, we became acquainted with the ladies and gentlemen of the China Inland Mission, of whom Mr. Judd is the pastor. These toilers in God's vineyard, for the better carrying out of their work, adopt the Chinese national dress. The ladies are young, seemingly, for such work, but possess unbounded enthusiasm.

Their visits to the ships were frequent, but not the less welcome in consequence; and long before we left we had got to look upon them as very dear friends. On one occasion they provided a temperance entertainment for as many as could come in the Seamen's Hall, on shore—a real floral fête, where the fair English faces of the ladies seemed to vie with the lovely blossoms around. There were many in that audience who went there under the impression of being bored, but who, long before the proceedings had finished, declared they had not enjoyed so pleasant an evening since leaving home. That was it, these kind Christian friends made that gathering so home-like, that one could scarce fail to be happy. For a few short hours only we rough sailors were permitted to enjoy the refined and cultured society of our generous friends, and it is to be hoped we came out the purer for the contact.

June 24th—The sweetest pleasure has its after-pang; the most beautiful rose its latent thorn. So, too, I see, is it with those who undertake to narrate facts. This day marks the loss of another shipmate, from one of those suddenly awful deaths to which the sailor is, above all other men, perhaps, ever liable, One of our boys, William Edwards, whilst at work on the main crosstrees, fell to the deck, sustaining such fearful injuries that he died a few moments afterwards. We buried him in the little cemetery on shore, where an unpretending gothic cross now records the simple fact that a sailor has died.

After all, our ship is not entirely useless; so thinks the admiral, for he left orders that we were to repair to Wosung to fill up with provisions for the squadron, and from thence to proceed to Nagasaki to await their arrival; a feat we performed, I believe, to his entire satisfaction.

Another of our old officers left us here to take command of the "Lapwing," her captain having shot himself in consequence of the decision of the court against him in the affair of the late collision. Much regret was felt at losing Mr. Haygarth—about the last of the executive officers who commissioned us.

Sometime after the sailing of the squadron, we left, with the "Zephyr" in company, to rejoin the admiral in Posiette Bay, Siberia. But the little ship being minus several sheets of copper, we put in at the island of Tsusima to allow her effective repairs.

August 7th.—And now we may be said to form a component part of the squadron; henceforth, the ships are to follow our lead, for the St. George's cross once more flutters from our fore-royal mast head.

Posiette is certainly a magnificent anchorage, capable of accommodating many fleets. All around richly clothed hills, admirably suited for grazing and agricultural purposes, shelter the great sheet of water from all winds. Nature, however, seems to hold undivided sway on those still, solemn hills, or those broad glassy plains; for not an animal nor house to betray the presence of the universal devastator can be seen, though I hear that only a short distance over the hills several thousands of Russian soldiers are under canvas, pending the conclusion of negociations with China, relative to Kashgar.

August 11th.—At noon the squadron, comprising the following ships: "Iron Duke," "Comus," "Encounter,"

"Curaçoa," "Pegasus," "Albatross," "Zephyr," and "Vigilant," were signalled to get under sail, except our ship, the "Zephyr," and the "Vigilant." Unfortunately for the accomplishment of this evolution, the wind, after holding out hopes that it would last all day, with the force of the morning fell light just as the ships had tripped their anchors. The little "Zephyr," in this emergency, proved of invaluable service. She was here, there, and everywhere to the rescue of her great sisters, which could not be induced anyhow to come to the wind. We were over four hours clearing the harbour, and even then steam had to be got up for the purpose.

Next day we reached Vladivostock, anchoring in a semicircle in front of the town. Scarce had our anchor left the bows when another of our young lads, William McGill, was suddenly ushered into that unknown world that lies beyond. Whilst uncovering the mizen gaff, he lost his hold, fell, and was so shattered that he died ere he could be borne below. He lies in the Russian cemetery on shore, a wild, neglected, "God's acre," without any pretensions to the sanctity usual to such places. Another of the "Iron Duke's" crosses, of stout old English oak, also marks this spot.

I must now request the reader to take a leap with me—permissible enough to book writers, though scarcely possible to pedestrians. You are now in the straits of Tsugar, and near the scene of our former misadventure. Before you are the ships of the squadron drawn up in line for a race—no, not all, for the "Mosquito" parted company during the night through stress of weather. The breeze is now blowing at force eight; or, as we should say, "slashing." During the night we had met with a few casualties to our sails, but so slight were they that in the morning we were able to take our place among the coursers, as judge, referee, and starter. At this moment the admiral signals "chase to windward." What takes place now is a pretty sight. Clouds of snowy balloon-like canvas spring, as if by magic, to masts and yards, straining and bellying out with tremendous effort. The steel corvettes were able to carry all plain sail with impunity. Not so with the "Encounter," however, for she is obliged to take a reef in her topsails and to furl her royals, a proceeding which does not lessen her chance of coming in first in the slighest, for she is known to be such a good sailer, that a few yards of canvas, more or less, does not affect her much. Away they go, listing over under the strong pressure, and rising and falling in all the majesty of ships of war. The "Pegasus" now shoots ahead, bidding fair to overhaul the corvettes, but her ambition is speedily curbed by the springing of her maintopsail yard. Placed *hors de combat*, she drops astern to shift her wounded spar. Many little accidents such as this, calling for prompt seamanship, occurred during the forenoon, and hence the value of such trials of speed.

For eight hours the squadron disported themselves in this manner, when the "Encounter" was declared the winner by 400 yards. At the moment of shortening sail our lame duck, the "Mosquito," hove in sight astern, in a sad plight, as is usual with lame ducks. She had lost her fore-topmast and jib-boom during the night, off O'Kosiri. She was at once signalled to repair to Hakodadi with all speed, to effect repairs.

By the time the race was finished we were broad off Hakodadi, on the opposite side of the strait, but as it was not intended to push on until next day, easy sail was kept on until daylight.

September 7th.—At daybreak a man-of-war, with the Japanese royal standard at the main—sky blue, with a white chrysanthemum in the centre—was observed making out of Hakodadi. Our larger ships at once saluted, the smaller ones lowering their upper sails at the same time. Subsequently we fell in with a Japanese squadron, all with royal flags displayed. They were in attendance on the mikado, who is now on a tour of his empire.

By the evening we had arrived and anchored in a double line, at right angles with the town.

We have, doubtless, all seen, heard, or read of the various devices adopted by the different peoples of the globe in the capture of the finny tribe, from our own familiar hook and line to the Chinaman's trained cormorant or the Chenook Indian's tame seal. These are all good in their way, only they involve a great loss of time and require no end of patience. But the method illustrated to us the morning after our arrival, besides being a more certain is also less cruel than anything else in the shape of fishing I have yet seen. Observing a vast quantity of fish disporting themselves near the ship, our experimental torpedo officer armed himself with a small torpedo, pulled himself into their midst, quietly dropped the missile overboard, and pulled away again. The beautiful unsuspecting creatures still played on, unconscious of the doom that awaited them. The effect on firing the torpedo was terrible: for a space of 150 yards all around, the surface was like one mass of silver, from the closely-packed and upturned bellies of a species of pilchard. The slaughter was complete—not a fish moved after the awful stun it had received. Boats from the squadron were signalled to gather up the slain, which will perhaps convey a pretty fair idea of their number.

Of late the admiral's barge has been attracting much attention by her sailing qualities. She has been taken in hand by the same energetic officer previously alluded to, who has altered the service rig, and provided a new set of sails, more suited in every way to develop the boat's qualities. We had not long to wait for a challenge, for the "Comus'" people, ever jealous in all such matters, offered to match their sailing pinnace against her. The challenge was accepted, and bets were concluded in the customary manner. The admiral, in particular, was especially pleased to think that, at last, he would have an opportunity of verifying his remarks about his boat; for he has reiterated again and again that, in his opinion, the boat wanted only proper handling to go. Well, as you know the race came off, and as you may also remember the "Comus'" boat was beat—in common phrase—"all to smash."

September 15th.—Southward once again. It was intended to call in at Yamada on the way down, but by some unaccountable reason we overshot the mark and found ourselves in Kama-ichi instead. The mistake was, of course, speedily discovered; the squadron hove around and headed north for Yamada.

Next we put in to Sendai bay, a commodious anchorage,

but very much exposed seaward from its broad and unprotected mouth. Great rollers and heavy swells come thundering in with nearly all winds.

Previous to leaving, the admiral conveyed his intention that certain ships would prepare to take the others in tow. Acting on this the "Curaçoa" took us and the "Mosquito;" the "Comus," the "Albatross" and "Zephyr;" and the "Swift," the "Lily." Thus we started, and under these conditions logged five knots, and all went merry until the sky began to frown, and displayed evident signs of bad temper. Half a gale blew, ships still towing, but cutting a violent caper because their freedom of action was curtailed. With the night the wind increased to a full gale, and as the ships were making the most frantic efforts to free themselves from the imprisoning hawsers, and likely to become bad friends over the job, signal was made to cast off. Now in her impatience the "Mosquito" was not content to wait until we gave her her freedom, but proceeded to wrest herself free by pulling one arm of our main bitts clean off to the deck. Annoying, was it not? But this is a quality generally conceded to mosquitoes I believe. The squadron now re-formed under reefed canvas, and though we could see scarcely 400 yards ahead, from the obscurity of the weather, we managed to reel off eight and a half knots, the "Duke" of course under steam.

Very cold and bleak blew the ice-cold breath of Fusi this morning as we headed into the bay of Yedo. Contrary to all our expectations, instead of making our way at once to Yokohama we turned aside, and anchored at the naval arsenal of Yokusuka, on the opposite side of the bay, presumably for the pupose of making the ships presentable to the argus-eyed naval critics in Yokohama.

On the 24th we slipped across in gallant style, and confessedly in first-rate order and trim. Even the "Yanks" conceded this, with a rider, of course, to the effect that they "guess'd" the "Alert"—did'nt they mean the "Palos," I wonder—"would knock saucepans out of the whole bilin'." On account of the great number of men-of-war already at anchor we had to take up stations as most convenient. As the flagship's anchor dropped, a signal from main, mizen, and yard-arms, drew the attention of the squadron. This great display of fluttering pennants and parti-colored squares conveys to the initiated the following sentence: "cruise at an end; satisfactory to both officers and men."

September 28th.—Before the dispersal of the ships to their winter quarters, and as a pleasant finale to an unpleasant cruise a regatta, under the sole patronage of the admiral and officers, was to be held on this and the two succeeding days. The two first days were allotted to the pulling contests, the third day to the sailing boats. Of the pulling races it will, perhaps, suffice to say that they were contested in the usual close and lusty manner.

The morn of the third day came in most auspiciously, so far as the wind was concerned; but by mid-day heavy rain clouds began to darken the weather horizon, and by their aspect, threatened to mar the pleasure of the proceedings. The race, however, had started long before this. More than ordinary excitement was felt concerning it, as the prize was to be a splendid silver cup, presented by the admiral, and which he hoped—which we too hoped, nay, confidently expected—would be won by his own boat. So beyond question it would had the breeze held. But it didn't, it fell to a flat calm, with not a breath to ripple the harbour's glassy surface. In some manner to wipe out their late defeat, and by a persistency really most laudable, the " Comus' " men *rolled* their pinnace all around the course, and ended by winning the cup. Some idea of the labour entailed on her crew may be formed from the time at which they were at it. At 10 a.m. the boats started, and it was not until 5 p.m. the race finished ; the crews being all this time without a drop of water, and under a vertical sun.

October 9th.—We are now in Nagasaki and about to go in dry dock on the morrow.

If we had previously made up our minds to any enjoyment in Japan's westernmost port we were doomed to disappointment, for we had not been an hour in the bay before alarming accounts reached us of the prevalence of a most virulent cholera on shore. Leave is of course out of the question—provoking, to say the least of it, in lovely Nagasaki. The captain at once issued a memo., couched in terms which ought to have appealed to each man's common sense, and containing the most accurate information with regard to the epidemic. In the face of all this, and notwithstanding the British consul's statistics, our men would not believe in the urgency of the case at all ; and several, despite all that could be urged against it crossed over to the town.

The days in dock were not, however, allowed to pass altogether unpleasantly or devoid of interest, for the officers—no whit better off than we in the matter of leave

—recognising the necessity of making an effort to divert ennui, and to set an example of cheerfulness under depressing circumstances, got up a series of athletic sports on the limited space afforded by the dock. It will suffice to notice a few of the leading items in our highly amusing programme, for amusing it really was from beginning to end, exemplifying to the letter the committee's motto, "fun, not dollars," though dollars were not lacking.

The sports commenced at 1 p.m. on the 13th, with a closely contested flat race of 100 yards. A sack race which followed was, of course, rare fun, though not to some who took the most active part in it, for I am afraid one's nose coming in contact with hard gravel is anything but fun to the owner of such organ. The jockey race which came next must be noticed as exhibiting steeds in entirely a new light. In the present instance, they so far threw aside the nature of the equine race that, they selected for themselves jockeys from the arms of fearful Japanese mothers, who had come to see the fun. Clearly, as the referees decided, this class of jockey did not come within the scope of the programme.

But one of the most entertaining items was the obstacle race, and considering, as I said before, the small space at the committee's command, several severe obstacles had been placed in the way of the competitors. Eighteen entered for this race. First, half a pound of pudding, minus anything oleaginous, and a basin of water was administered to each. At a given signal the "gorging" commenced. He who first got outside his "duff and water" started, and so on with the next. One would scarce believe with what incredible rapidity that pudding was metamorphosed. The next obstacle to be surmounted was a huge balk of timber raised at the ends, about a foot off the ground, under which the coursers were compelled to *crawl*. A row of eighteen barrels, with the ends knocked out, came next; then a climb up slack ropes, and over a transverse bar; and finally another balk of timber—if anything less than a foot off the ground—under which they had to squeeze and wriggle in the best manner possible.

As a finale to our excellent programme, the most amusing and entertaining thing of all was yet to be carried out. A stunsail boom had been rigged out over the caisson, and rendered extremely fit for pedestrianism by plentiful libations of slush and soft soap. At the extreme end a basket containing, in the words of the programme, "a little pig" was slung. About thirty men stood to the front, as would-be possessors of "porcus." Each of the thirty, as valiant heroes as ever trod a plank or fisted handspike, tried and failed—and tried again with a like unsatisfactory result. Piggy still lay nestled in his swinging stye. True, once or twice he had cocked out his head with an enquiring squeal as the pole now and then received an extra hard shake, making the foundations of his house rather insecure. The affair was at length decided in an unlooked-for manner. As the thirty could not get the pork out, the latter took the initiative and got out himself—of course falling overboard, where he was secured by an amphibious sailor below.

As the time anticipated had not been consumed in the pork affair, a tug-of-war between the fore and aft men was decided on; and as it is a generally understood thing that our men can pull on occasions, a four-and-half hemp hawser was hauled to the front, experience having proved that ropes of lesser diameter are like as much tow in their hands. As no prize could be conveniently awarded for this, about six dollars' worth of that ambiguous compound, known as gingerbread, was supplied and laid on a piece of canvas in a formidable heap within view of the antagonists, with the intention that the winners might regale themselves afterwards. But this highly laudable and very proper intention was frustrated, for the *losers* happening to be nearest the heap took base advantage of their proximity to pillage the store, which, by the aid of a score or so of Japanese imps, in all manners of reversible attitudes in the crowd, they managed to raze to its foundations. So ended one of the most enjoyable days of the commission.

By the way I must not omit to mention that the ubiquitous "Aunt Sally," of immortal memory, was present on the occasion, and contributed the usual amount of sport.

October 14th.—By midnight, all hands having relegated themselves to the close embraces of the sleepy god, a terrible din and an unusual alarm was circulated throughout the ship. At first, in our semi-wakeful state, and before we could adjust our ideas, we had the most confused notions of what was the matter. Most thought that the shores under the ship's bottom had carried away, and that we had fallen over on our bilge; and, strange to say, in our imaginary terror our eyes seemed to convey that impression. The ominous word "fire!" followed by the maddening unmusical efforts of a crazed bell, reduced all this din and uncertainty to a logical something. But where was it? What was on fire, the ship? Fortunately no; but a fire so close to the ship that she was in imminent danger of taking the flames every minute. Ahead of us, and within a biscuit's throw of our flying boom, a long shed containing kerosene and other inflammables had taken fire, but how does not so clearly appear. But that doesn't matter. In a moment there was a general conflagration. It burst out with sudden and alarming fierceness, threatening speedily to overwhelm the whole yard.

Our captain's first consideration was the safety of his ship. To this end the dock was flooded, and pumps rigged on board in readiness for any possible eventuality; for, though we were not in immediate contact with the danger, yet it was so unpleasantly hot on our top-gallant forecastle, and such quantities of sparks and lumps of burning wood were so constantly lodging on our tarry ropes and rigging, that there was no saying how soon we too might add to the general glare.

The means for putting out fires in Japan are, as everybody knows, of the most simple and primitive kind. But simple and ineffective as their method is, we were compelled to adopt it until there should be a sufficiency of water in the dock to enable us to work our pumps. One would have thought that in a Government yard like this the machinery for pumping out the dock might have been utilized for such a purpose. Possibly if fires were of less frequent occurrence amongst the Japanese this plan might be considered.

After the ship had been attended to we next turned our

attention to the fire. From the first we saw it was useless to attempt its subjugation, even had we the ordinary appliances at hand, so our efforts were mainly directed to the prevention of its spreading to another shed standing near, containing vitriol, and to the preservation of a stack of huge balks of timber, adjoining the burning shed. We succeeded in the former, but the timber proved too cumbrous to be interfered with, and it was not until four o'clock in the morning that the fire was got under—or rather, burnt itself out is, I suppose, the more correct expression. After a good hour and half's delay a Japanese fire brigade arrived on the scene. The appearance of this body of men was such that they claim a few words of description. They were attired in tight-fitting blue garments, and mushroom-shaped hats of bamboo, with each an umbrella over his shoulder, the use of which will become apparent directly. Before the cortege marched a man blowing a large conch, which emitted, not "the murmur of the shell," but a much more ear-splitting music. Next to him came a personage bearing the insignia —I suppose we must term it—of the brigade. This affair reminded me of nothing at home so much as the stall or stand of the itinerant vendor of boot and corset laces in our streets, the laces in this case being represented by strips of gilded leather, and surmounted by a ball, on which was traced a great character in gold, signifying fire, in the language of the children of the "rising sun." Then followed their box-like engine, borne on bamboos across the shoulders of the main body. Notwithstanding the ludicrousness of the whole cavalcade, the men set to work most energetically, and displayed that dash and intrepidity of conduct for which the Japanese are famed, and which must eventually raise them to the dominance of the peoples of the far east. Right into the midst of the fire dashed these fellows, their only shelter from the fierce glare being the before-mentioned umbrellas. These frail shades, though made only of paper, seemed to answer the purpose admirably.

October 26th.—Left for Wosung, anchoring in the Yang-tsze, after a quick run of four days across the Yellow Sea. We are to await here the arrival of the flying squadron. Meanwhile an opportunity was given us of visiting the great European metropolis of China. The "Foxhound" was ordered down from Shanghai, and converted into a passenger steamer, for the benefit of our ship's company. Shanghai at this time offered plenty of scope for enjoyment to sailors. The city is divided into three principal parts or "concessions"—English, French, and American—the English being far more extensive than the other two combined, and much more beautiful, with clean broad streets, houses like palaces, and shops which would do no discredit to Regent street or the Strand. The great attraction was the races, held outside the city, on the Nankin Road, near which is an extensive race-course.

Of the native city—well—perhaps the less said the better. It is full of the foulest filth and abominations in which it is possible for even a Chinaman to exist. I will not afflict my readers with a description of its horrors; it would scarcely be fit reading for our friends. Fever and plague are ever rife within the city gates, a fact so well established that the European residents never visit this quarter. We had not been warned of this, however, and the result was that some of our men, who had weakened their systems with poisonous liquor, fell victims to some disease very like cholera, which in two cases proved fatal within twenty-four hours. I trust these awfully terrible examples were not without their lesson to us. (Shipmates, there is a higher aspiration within the reach of every sailor than that of blindly devoting himself to the service of the "boozy" god, a self-immolation which leaves no enjoyment—no healthy enjoyment, I mean—to its devotees. It must be, and I know it is so, that every one such feels ashamed of himself afterwards, and calls himself by hard but honest adjectives when the "bad head" period comes on.) I am thankful to state that our other cases recovered, though not until almost all hope had well-nigh gone.

November 22nd.—To-day the long-expected flying squadron arrived, and took up positions ahead of us. The following ships comprised it—"Inconstant" (flag), "Bacchante," "Cleopatra," "Tourmaline," and "Carysfort."

For days past much activity has existed amongst the junk fleet in this neighbourhood. Dozens of these trim-built and picturesque-looking craft have lately accumulated here to give the princes a proper reception. Day after day they have duly gone through some extraordinary and to us meaningless evolutions, all flags, gongs, yells, and gunpowder.

November 24th.—Leaving the squadron to the joy and festivities of Shanghai, once more we head for Hong Kong. We thought then it was for the last time; but hopes have been shattered so frequently of late that we were not prepared to bet on it.

Whilst at anchor, awaiting the tide to cross the outer bar, our attendant pilot boat came to grief under our bows. Everybody who knows anything of Chinese rivers—of the Yangtsze in particular—will have often remarked how great a velocity the current attains at near low water, making boating alongside a ship an almost impossible and extremely hazardous proceeding. The water hisses, seethes, and boils past the sides as if the ship was under weigh in a heavy sea; thus when the little vessel reached our bows there was nothing to save her. Fortunately she came down upon us in such a manner that she escaped with the loss of mainmast and sail, whilst a little damage was done to our head-gear in the scrimmage.

November 30th.—Again the well-known rig of the Canton fishing junks heaves in sight, and ere long the equally well-known outline of Victoria Peak, the most welcome sight on the station, after all said and done. In a few hours that prince of bumboat men, old Attam, had paid us a visit, giving us a kindly welcome, with his good-tempered, ever-smiling, and flat celestial face.

December 20th.—To-day at noon the flying squadron came in from the northward. Their arrival was awaited by eager and expectant crowds thronging the shore, in anticipation of witnessing the landing of the young royal middies. In this they were disappointed. The same absence of ceremony and reserve was to be observed here, with respect to the queen's grandsons, as was recently followed out in Shanghai, and which gave so much umbrage to the residents of that city. It was soon officially known that whilst staying at Hong Kong, the princes would be publicly recognised simply as " mids."

The Europeans and other foreign residents were quite prepared to do the honors handsomely, had things been ordered differently. These shortcomings were however amply compensated for by the magnificence of the Chinamen. It did not signify to them as to *how* the princes were to be treated; to them they were the queen's grandsons, midshipmen or not.

The two nights immediately preceding Christmas Day were devoted to the grandest display of fireworks and illuminations I have ever witnessed, and which, possibly, few men see but once in a lifetime. All accounts of China agree that in the pyrotechnic art the Chinese stand alone, unequalled.

We have all, no doubt, been struck when reading of the wonderful changes of form assumed by their fireworks in the air. This, like many other descriptions about this people, is rather misleading. What actually does take place I will endeavour to show; only bear in mind the most perfect description must fall far short of the startling reality.

In the present instance two skeleton, tower-like structures of bamboo were erected in the soldiers' drill ground, and within this simple framework all the business was to be transacted. Seats for the accommodation of the governor and other high functionaries, and for the leading Chinese, were set up at a convenient distance, whilst the respectable public were permitted within the enclosure. For several hours before dusk, relays of coolies had been bearing into the open space curious-looking balls of wicker, innocent of anything like the gorgeous things they really were. At sunset the programme opened. One of the balls was hoisted to the top of a tower, and set fire to in its ascent, so that by the time it had reached its highest altitude it was all one blaze. But behold the change! so sudden and brilliant that a shout expressive of admiration was involuntarily sent up by the sea of faces around. In place of the homogenous ball, hundreds of small figures of mandarins and ladies, some seated at tables, some riding on mules, others playing at shuttlecock or flying kites, and all clothed in the most beautiful garments, and around which innumerable squibs were hissing and cracking, revealed themselves to our astonished gaze. Another change! The human element disappears. Birds and flowers, with swarms of brilliant butterflies flitting amongst them, and alighting on their gorgeous petals, the light all the time ever-changing and varying in color. These in their turn disappear, and a grand pagoda suddenly drops, as from the skies, out of the burning mass, its different storys all distinctly marked by parti-colored lamps, whilst little rockets are continually going off at all its windows. What, not finished yet? No; exit pagoda, enter a royal crown, dominating the Prince of Wales' feathers, with the initials "A V" and "G" underneath. Bear in mind all these changes emanated from the *same* ball, which was but one of scores such, and all different. Each ball generally wound up in one tremendous report, and a rocket, which shot far into the night, and whose sparks, scintillating for awhile in space, rivalled in brilliancy the tints of the stars.

This was but the first part of the entertainment; a far prettier was yet to come. Starting from the various Chinese guilds, and uniting in front of the governor's house, a grand procession, over a mile long, commenced the perambulation of the streets of the city. Each man bore on his shoulders exaggerated representations of all the domestic and food animals used in the Chinese mènage, principally fish, fowls, and pigs, constructed of bamboo framework covered with tinted gauze, and illumined from within by colored candles. Illuminated shops, trophies, interiors, representations in character from the sacred books, the figures being real and resplendent in the most beautiful silks, were amongst the most important objects in the ceremonial. Bands of music—save the mark!—filled up the intervals. Towards the end of the procession came two dragons—a gold one and a silver one—of such a length that each required somewhere about thirty pairs of bearers. They were divided into sections, to every one of which a pair of men was attached, illumined from within, and covered with a rich scaled brocade, in which the bearers themselves were also enveloped, their legs and feet appearing from underneath like the legs of a huge centipede.

Whilst on the subject of dragons I may just mention a curious ceremony I witnessed, during the earlier part of the day, in connection with one of these—the gold one—in the present ceremonial. The occasion was the instillation of life into the legendary monster. He was conducted by his bearers to the largest temple in the city, where a yellow-robed bonze was in waiting to receive him. On the huge head being brought to the door the farce commenced. Taking a live cock in his hand, the priest pricked its comb in three several places, and with the blood proceeded to mix some vermilion paint, in a small china vessel. With this pigment he now described three cabalistic signs on a piece of yellow paper, which he stuck on the monster's forehead, at the same time touching with his brush the eyes, the cavernous jaws, and horrible fangs of the animal. This completes the business, and the dragon proceeds on its sinuous way amidst the howling and contortions of a superstitious and excited mob.

It is not to be supposed that the flying squadron could be permitted to leave for England without the usual challenges for boating contests being thrown out. We, of course, came in for the lion's share of their attacks. A match was pulled, in which our green galley came in the victor; then a second, in which the "Bacchante's" cutter beat our crack boat. This unexpected defeat set our men on their metal, in fact raised a bit of a storm in the lower deck, so that dollars were freely tendered towards a high stake to pull them again. But the "Bacchante" wanted not our two hundred dollars. "They had beat us," they said, "and to their entire satisfaction; what more could they desire?" The "Tourmaline's" men appeared highly delighted at our defeat. On a black board, fixed up in their fore-rigging, they had written, "'Iron Duke' no can do 'Bacchante.'" This was met by a counter taunt from us, "'Iron Duke' can do 'Bacchante'—200 dollars." I am inclined to the belief that had the "Dukes" and "Tourmalines" met on shore that night there would have been work for the doctors.

CHAPTER XV.

Heave, heave, heave ! around the capstan,
Up with the anchor with a will ;
For the "Duke," you may rely,
Will be home by next July,
If you'll only put old *Tom Lee* to the wheel.

THE SECOND CRUISE OF THE CHINA SQUADRON.—PRINCIPALLY CONCERNING A VISIT TO THE LOO-CHOO ISLES AND COREA.—WELCOME NEWS FROM HOME.—CONCLUSION.

BEFORE starting for the north, suppose we just glance at a few of the leading events which transpired at the beginning of the year. The flying squadron has sailed after having awaited the return of the "Inconstant" from docking at Nagasaki.

The arrival of the yacht "Wanderer" must also be noted; for Mr. Lambert, her princely owner, gave a magnificent cup worth 200 dollars as a prize to be sailed for by the boats of the men-of-war in harbour. It was borne off by the French admiral's barge.

In stripping our yards serious defects were discovered in the fore and main, necessitating the replacing of the latter by a new one, and the splicing of the former. Whilst awaiting these repairs the admiral hurried us off, stripped as we were, up the Canton river to a bleak open spot above the Bogue forts. The scenery of the river is flat and uninviting, but eminently characteristic. Almost every hill has its pagoda at the top, every bank that peculiar fishing apparatus—a lever net, and the river is swarming with great lumbering junks, not a few of which, if rumour speak correctly, engaged in piracy.

On the way up we obtained a fine view of the Bogue forts. The old ruins still remain, mute witnesses of the completeness of our cannonade during the Chinese war. At a short distance from the old, a much stronger and more formidable structure is reared, which in the hands of Europeans would form an almost impassable barrier. In addition to the large fort, two small islands off in the river are also strongly fortified with eighteen-ton guns.

Ten days—such was the term of our banishment. Economically considered, I suppose it was all right; no doubt the fresh water of the river succeeded in removing the saline incrustations from our bottom. One of the home papers, more sensationally than truthfully, remarked that our ship's company were all such a disreputable, boosing set, and proved themselves so reckless and recalcitrant when on shore, that the admiral took this means of punishing us. Now I call this a gross libel on the ship's company at large. To speak honestly, I don't believe the admiral did send us here for such a purpose, nor do I believe we are one whit worse than those who stigmatize our characters in so wholesale and careless a manner.

Next in order of events comes the admiral's inspection

—searching, of course, as all his inspections are known to be. He has a curious knack of catching people on what, in lower-deck phrase, is styled the "ground-hop," and generally succeeds, by his rapid and pertinent questions, in putting people into such utter confusion of ideas that negatives and affirmatives are bundled out indiscriminately, if indeed the mouth can be induced to open itself at all, or to frame any speech. However, in one department, at least, he got as good as he gave. Whilst visiting the magazine he suddenly gave the order, "fire on the flat!" The gunner's mate in charge of the magazine, whom we will call "Topper," immediately closed the hatch and stood on guard over it. Turning around, the admiral said "I want to go into the magazine;" but observing that "Topper" still stood motionless, he again repeated the order. "You can't, sir," was the rejoinder, "because there is fire in the flat." "Oh! very well," replied the admiral, "cease fire!" With great promptitude and despatch the hatch was removed, and the admiral prepared to descend, but was once more checked, and was informed that if he complied with the magazine regulations, and left his shoes and sword behind, he might do so. He fared no better down below, I believe, and left the magazine perfectly satisfied with the conduct of affairs in that region.

A few days before sailing, a suggestion made by Mr. Robinson, the officer whose kindnesses I have had occasion to note before, met with universal favor. For a very small sum each man, a telegram was sent to Mr. R——'s agent in London, in the following words—"When will 'Audacious' commission, and probably sail?" For three days nothing else was spoken of, and various were the speculations as to the answer. It came—"Early September." Very short, but to the point, though to some rather ambiguous. To which did the answer refer, the *commissioning*, or the *sailing?* Reason implied the former, as, knowing it, the latter might be inferred. A subsequent telegram set the matter at rest.

April 19th.—After a more than ordinarily long stay at Hong Kong, to-day sees us clearing out of the harbour on our projected summer cruise. The following ships besides ourselves comprised the squadron—"Curaçoa," "Encounter," "Albatross," "Swift," "Daring," and "Foxhound," with the "Vigilant" and "Zephyr," which accompanied us out of the harbour. On parting company with the admiral we shaped course for Manilla, the admiral being specially careful to give Captain Tracey injunctions not to forget to bring him 2,000 cigars from that place. We were then sailing under sealed orders.

April 24th.—This morning, having sent the "Swift" back to Hong Kong, the sealed orders were opened, and, to the surprise of everybody—to the captain's not less than to our own—we were not to go to Manilla at all! This in the face of what the admiral said to the captain! Well, up helm, and away we go for Loo-Choo; it does not signify much where we go for the next six or eight months, I suppose.

April 25th.—*Caught our first shark.* Yes; one out of the many scores in the vicinity actually meditated an attack on our four-pound piece. However he discovered, to his cost, that a barbed hook is no easy matter to digest. He was landed inboard in a trice, and handed over to the tender mercies of the forecastle hands. Now it was a most unfortunate thing for that shark that one of these same *tender* hands had, that very morning, lost a "hook pot" of fish off the range, through the kind services of some obliging shipmate. Hence revenge was the dominant feeling in that man's breast. Electing himself butcher-in-chief, sharko's spirit was soon gathered to his fathers.

A most devilish contrivance—torpedo, electric wire, and all complete—was invented by our torpedo officer for the accommodation of the next friendly shark. With this little affair safely stowed within his stomach, he would find his internal arrangements subject to sudden and unaccountable tension. Enough this to make the shark parliament pass a bill condemning all illicit grabbing.

April 20th.—Off the east of Formosa, and during the middle watch, the ships of the squadron were caught aback in a sudden squall. There was a deuce of a commotion up aloft, sails flapping and splitting, ropes cracking, and blocks rattling till further orders. To establish order amongst these refractory things the hands were called. Next day the wind crept ahead and gradually freshened to what looked and felt extremely like a gale. The poor little "Foxhound" had a lively time of it, and proved herself unequal to such a buffetting. The "Curaçoa" was signalled to take her in tow, and the two fell rapidly astern, and finally disappeared, to rejoin us about the third day afterwards. On May first the "Daring" parted company for Napa, the capital of Great Loo-Choo, our destination being Little Loo-Choo.

May 3rd.—I don't know if we do, but sailors ought to feel it a great privilege that they are enabled to see all the wonderful and varied sights so constantly surrounding them—the many countries and people they come in contact with. Of all strange, out of the way, scarce heard of places, perhaps, Loo-Choo has been less subject to the visits of vandals from Europe than any. If I am correctly informed it is now close on thirty years since a ship of war put in to Little Loo-Choo, and certainly never before such a squadron as the present.

But two visits of consequence have taken place during the present century; that of Captain Maxwell in the "Alceste," in 1817; and that of Commodore Perry, of the U.S. navy, in 1853; so that the little we do know of this *ultima thule* is derivable from these sources. Strangely enough, the two accounts are broadly opposed to each other. Captain Maxwell found the people gentle, simple, and courteous; possessed of no money, no arms, without police, or punishments; whilst the land, he said, was an earthly paradise. I have in my possession an old print entitled "the voyage of the 'Alceste,'" written by the surgeon of that ship; and that part of it which refers to this visit is most pleasurable reading. The commodore, on the other hand, endeavours to shew many of Captain Maxwell's eulogies to be erroneous. It is certain, says he, that the Loo-Chooans possess and understand the use of both money and arms; and that they have a very severe and cruel code of punishment. So far as we are able, let us judge which of the two descriptions comes nearest the truth.

The Loo-Choo group of islands lies in the North Pacific, and forms a semi-circle, extending from Japan to the island of Formosa. The inhabitants number under three millions, perhaps. The two principal islands of the group are known as Great and Little Loo-Choo. It is to the latter that the following remarks must be understood to refer. This island is almost intersected by a narrow arm of the sea reaching far, far away inland amongst the richly clad hills and mountains. This, according to the charts, is Hancock bay, up which we are steaming. Nature is looking her best as we pass, and wafting off to us her sweetest smells; a green summer mantle clothes every eminence and gentle slope; and the nestling villages have such a quiet, peaceful look, that it seems almost a pity to disturb them—as we certainly shall—from their dream-like repose. Each village possesses its water mill or mills, so that the natives are not entirely ignorant of mechanics.

Hundreds of canoes, of the rudest construction, crammed with men, women, and children, put off to us when we came to anchor. Though it is said they are of mixed Chinese and Aïno origin; the people are of cast countenance, and style of dress peculiar to the Japanese; they have, however, a way of doing their hair, all their own. The men gather all theirs into a tuft at the poll, where it is secured with a silk marling, the extreme ends forming a sort of fringe, like a plume of feathers. The very fine, long, and glossy hair of the women is rolled jauntily on the top of the head in a loose spiral coil, resembling the volutes of a shell. Through this rather graceful head-dress they stick a long silver pin, in some cases a foot long.

They appear a very timid race. This is particularly noticeable on board. Whether it was because they saw none of their own sex amongst us, I know not; but I doubt if the women saw much of what they had come to see, as most of their time was passed in eclipse under their husbands' lee, and whose hands they never once loosed from the time of entering the ship until they left us again. We treated them to sailors' fare, allowing them the free run of our bread barges, and endeavoured all we could—but without success—to set them at their ease They were all highly perfumed with the penetrating odour of garlic. I noticed that the married ladies, in common with Aïno women, tattoo the backs of their hands, though not their mouths.

One king generally suffices a people,—and even one is often found too much—but this race tolerates *three*, or did until very recently; one of their own; the emperor of China, whom they call father; and the mikado of Japan, whom they style mother. To both their "parents" they pay an immense tribute, which annually absorbs two-thirds of their produce. It will be inferred from this that the condition of the lower classes is very unfavorable.

Since we have been on this station these islands have been a bone of contention, between China and Japan, as to which shall possess them; the old "father" and "mother" farce being recognised as played out by mutual consent. The Japs, in 1877, took the initiative, and sent an expedition to Napa, and forcibly made the native king prisoner; and before the Chinese were aware of what was taking place, the Japanese were administering the laws in all parts of the little kingdom, and gradually absorbing it into their empire. The question between the two nations is far from being settled yet, and may at any future time prove a *casus belli*.

The appearance of the houses on shore has given rise to not a little speculation. All that we are enabled to make out of them from the ship is a thatched roof raised about ten feet off the ground, and supported on four stout uprights. Can these be dwelling houses? On landing, and coming close up with them, we at once saw that whatever else they were intended for, they were not places of abode. Close under the admirably palm thatched roof is a strongly-made, tray-shaped floor, with a small locked door beneath the eaves. Such was their simple structure. After a little thought, we arrived at the conclusion that they must be granaries for the stowage of grain, possibly the government tribute houses, as they were of different design and vastly superior build to the mud and stick hovels in which the people live. In their surroundings the natives exhibit all the squalor and dirt of China, with none of the cleanlier qualities of the people of Japan. Though they followed us about in droves, they never attempted any familiarities; in fact our first overtures were treated with awe-like silence. The only words we understood, in common with them, were "tabac" and "Ya-pun" (Japan); indeed Japan is the beginning and end of their ideas—their one standard of perfection. Everything they noticed about us— watches, biscuit, the buttons on our clothing, our *boots* even—were all qualified with the word "Ya-pun," in a most admiring and reverential tone. Seemingly the Loo-Chooans have never heard of England, though on passing a school house—wherein were about a score of children on their knees behind a similar number of box-like desks, one of the youngsters jumped up and shewed me an English spelling book!

We saw no money amongst them. They however recognised the Japanese silver yen, but more on account of the inscription on it than from any knowledge of its money value, I think. Buttons were eagerly sought after.

Their wants seem to be extremely few and simple; and being excellent agriculturists and expert fishers, the land and sea amply supply these demands. Their chief export is raw sugar. We noticed some women at rude looms engaged in manufacturing a coarse kind of cloth out of cocoa-nut fibre; but from its appearance most of their wearing apparel is of Japanese fabrication. The parents are very affectionate towards their children—who, by the way, don't trouble their mammas for more clothes than they were born in, until they are about seven or eight years old.

The earth teems with beautiful and profuse vegetation —for the most part in a wild state. Magnificent convolvuluses and lilies, rare ferns—of which I gathered, perhaps, as rare a collection—amongst them two or three species of tree ferns, great raspberries and gooseberries; and a very arcadia of flowers, lovely objects all for the artist's pencil.

The women seem devoid of that quality we so much admire in Englishwomen, and which is so rarely found beyond England's shores—the quality of modesty. It is rather embarrassing, for instance, whilst bathing to find your clothes—which you had left on the beach—the centre of an admiring and criticising crowd of ladies, handling and trying on each separate article of your rather intricate wardrobe, and wishing, no doubt, the owner would swim to shore and help them in their efforts. Such unaffected simplicity and ingenuousness is most refreshing to witness.

How extremely alike child nature is all over the world! Observing a little half-famished girl in a canoe alongside, I handed her a piece of jam tart through the port. At first she was at a loss what to do with it, but soon following out an universal law in such cases, she ventured to put it to her mouth. The result may be expected; for no matter how widely tastes differ, every child likes jam. It was real good to see the hearty way in which that copper-skinned maid smacked her tiny cherry lips, and looked her grateful thanks through her great lustrous almond eyes. With the intention, perhaps, of sharing the delicacy with her brothers and sisters, who shall say? she carefully wrapped up the remainder, and placed it inside her only garment. How often, dear reader, have you and I not done similarly at school feasts? Though this little Loo-Choo's heart was willing, the flesh was weak; the parcel was again taken out, re-examined, and re-tasted—but with evident reluctance—till, finally, after a few ineffectual efforts to overcome selfishness, the whole was consumed.

It is satisfactory to be able to write that in their dealings with this simple people our men acted always with kindness and consideration; paying, or offering payment —for it was generally refused—for everything they had.

The arrival of the "Swift" with our mails was the signal for our departure from pleasant Loo-Choo.

Perhaps it may be remembered that just about this time English society at home seems to have undergone a mental crisis which, at one time, certainly threatened the fabric of its reason; and all about that absurd pachyderm

"Jumbo." Of course, more or less, any agitation emanating from home must in time reach Englishmen abroad; thus the "Jumbo" wave visited these seas, and day after day, week after week, it was nothing but "Jumbo." You would have thought the whole ship's company was sickening for elephantiasis. Some funny fellow in the squadron noticing this weakness, attached the name to our ship which, amongst the blue jackets at least, has entirely supplanted the original one. But this by the way.

Well, we reached Nagasaki without accident; coaled, and left for Kobé,—south of Kiusiu—with a rattling breeze fair abaft. All went smoothly until we arrived off Satano-Misaki, the southernmost point of Kiusiu. The word "Satano," if it be, as is said, of Portuguese origin, needs no comment. Here the fine breeze forsook us, and left us in a flat and quite unexpected calm; for, generally speaking, in rounding this cape the reverse of calms is met with. To make matters still more unpleasant, a heavy ground swell began to set through the straits, and the squadron having fires drawn at the time we all found ourselves in the doldrums. Still, however, there was something of a current which had its effect on the ships, so that it was impossible to keep in anything like station. In this state of affairs the "Curaçoa" drifted on top of the "Daring," and cracked her up a bit, rendering extensive repairs to her absolutely necessary. She was despatched on to Kobé for this purpose.

After varying fortunes, now a calm—anon a gale, we arrived at Kobé on June 3rd. This makes the sixth time during the commission we have touched at this place, and strange coincidence! on fives times out of the six we have anchored at noon, and have dined off that delightful compound, pea-soup, on entering the harbour.

Meanwhile the admiral and the "Swift" are away in Corea, negociating a treaty with that nation.

On reaching Yokohama we found our anticipated pleasures doomed to disappointment; for that yearly visitant, cholera, was holding high revel in the town, and doing pretty well just as it pleased. Nevertheless, the admiral arrived the previous day, and gave leave to the squadron until 9 p.m., with injunctions against visiting certain localities.

A few days subsequently we were joined by the "Cleopatra," late of the flying squadron, but detached at Suez for service on this station. The "Comus," meanwhile, is about to leave for the Pacific to replace the "Champion," ordered to join our flag.

In spite of the precautions supposed to have been observed, cholera at length discovered itself in the fleet; and on the 27th June a case from the "Vigilant" and another from the "Encounter," were conveyed to the hospital. At once further restrictions were placed on the leave, and though not absolutely stopped it was curtailed to sundown.

July 2nd.—Resumed our cruise (now under the admiral) to the northward. The "Foxhound," outside, was signalled to repair to Hong Kong, and the "Zephyr" ordered up to take her place. The "Foxhound" has shewn herself to be a most indifferent sailer and steamer, and not at all suited as a handy auxiliary to the squadron.

July 5th.—Four years in commission to-day! Are we ever to hear anything of our relief ? I think we shall be preparing for eventualities if we meditate a serious study of the Chinese and kindred languages to fit us for an indefinite stay in the far east. Have they forgotten us at home?

On the passage to Hakodadi the "Cleopatra" and "Curaçoa" each lost a poor fellow, of cholera. Thus it is evident had we not cleared out of Yokohama when we did the epidemic might have taken alarming hold on the squadron.

We have left Hakodadi, and are now cruising up the gulf of Tartary to as far north as our first year's round. Passing by Dui we braced sharp up, encountering, with double reefs, a strong wind and heavy sea for the sixty miles stretch across to Castries bay, making that anchorage in a dense fog. Hence we recrossed to Dui, coaled, and continued southward to Barracouta harbour. For the future this anchorage will possess a melancholy interest for the "Cleopatra;" for, a day before sailing, the squadron was startled to hear that a shocking and fatal occurrence had happened to an officer of that ship, who was unfortunately shot through the inadvertent discharge of a fowlingpiece. He was an officer much beloved by the ship's company.

August 12th.—A day's sail from Vladivostock we fell in with the "Champion," one of the "Curaçoa" class. I suppose, from her appearance, black must be the uniform of the Pacific station, a color which looks confessedly proper and ship-shape, but one which our admiral will not allow on any account.

On arriving at Vladivostock, scraping operations were commenced on her, and by the following morning early her crew had greeted us with "Good-bye, 'Jumbo,'" which they had erased in great straggling letters along one broadside.

Our last mails, brought up by the "Zephyr," have narrowly escaped total destruction—at least such might have been the fate of one of them; for the steamer conveying it to Yokohama struck on a rock in the Inland Seas, and foundered—the mails being immersed for so long a period that when our letters reached us they were reduced to what Sala would call an "epistolary pulp." But no news came of the "Audacious," only what the poor mothers and wives say.

August 24th.—For the first time during our already long commission we are about to make an acquaintance with the "hermit kingdom"—that, I believe, is what one writer calls Corea. Japan has for a number of years held a sort of *quasi* intercourse with this country, and has even gone so far as to send an embassy to the court at Séoul, and to establish two or three settlements along the coast within the last two years. But the Coreans, taking their cue from their suzerain, China, have ever looked with a jealous eye on the Japanese and any other foreign relations. However, China's Bismarck, the astute Li-hung-Chang, has recently altered his tactics, and is now as anxious that Corea should enter into the community of nations as he was before, that it should stand outside; thus, when our admiral, at the beginning of the recent treaty, solicited the prime minister's aid it was readily given; for, argued he, what Corea, concedes to foreigners surely China has a right to demand.

Since we have been on this station two countries have

attempted to enter into treaty relations with Corea—the
" Vittor Pinani, for Italy, in 1880, and Commodore Shufeldt, for America, in the "Ticonderego," in the same year; but both, I believe, have resulted in failure—the first because, instead of the Italians calling China to their aid, they relied too much on the mediations of Japan, a nation whom the Coreans mortally detest: and the second because, though Li-hung-Chang was the medium, Corea, whilst admitting her inferiority to China, claimed equality with America, or with any other of the great civilized powers.

Of course no European nation is willing to concede so much; hence, for the present, that treaty is annulled. It remains to be seen if ours is a more honorable one or not.

At present Corea is in a state bordering on anarchy. Sundry rumours have reached us recently of some disturbance south. So far as I am able to glean, this is what is actually occurring. The late king dying without issue, his adopted son, the present king, ascended the throne. During his minority his father acted as regent—a position the latter found to suit him so well that, by-and-by, when his son became of age he refused to abdicate the throne in favor of its lawful occupant, threw off all semblance of allegiance, and assumed a high-handed and arrogant bearing, especially exhibited towards the queen and her family, with whom the regent was at bitter feud. To compass their destruction was then his first care, and he openly declared to the mutinous palace guard that their grievances would not be redressed until they had compassed the queen's death. He even suggested to them how they were to set about it—nay, even offered to aid them. On a certain night during last July, and according to previous arrangement, the soldiers repaired to the palace, shouting "the queen, death to the queen." That innocent lady, turning to her unnatural father-in-law, asked what the shouting meant and what the people wanted of her? and he, pretending to advise her for her good, told her that rather than live to be outraged by the soldiers it was better she should die by her own hand, at the same time placing a cup of poison before her, which she in her extremity actually drank, sharing it with her son's wife, a girl only eleven years old. The king was compelled to seek safety in flight, and according to last accounts is still in hiding.

The regent, now left master of the situation, next turned the people against the Japanese embassy, of whom there were twenty-eight in all. The subsequent adventures of this little band of brave men reads more like a page of a romance than a fact of to-day's occurrence. After fighting their way through immense odds—crossing rivers in open boats amidst flights of stones and arrows—lying down to rest, to find themselves, on awaking, surrounded by a revengeful and infuriated people—they at length reached the shore to find no junk or vessel of sufficient size to convey them across the narrow sea to their own country. Driven to face their enemies on the very verge of the ocean, they eventually succeeded in retreating to some small boats—in which, wounded and bleeding, but all alive, they confided themselves to the sea, as being more merciful than their relentless and cruel foe. All this, I say, savours of the romantic. Fortunately for the poor worn-out voyagers help was at hand, for soon H.M.S. "Flying Fish" hove in sight, on board which they were kindly received, and brought to Nagasaki.

These stirring events have actually occurred whilst we have been lying quietly at anchor, in Gen San and Chosan. Under such a state of affairs, who shall predict the fate of Admiral Willes' treaty?

I trust I may be pardoned for being thus prolix; but surely, we who are actually on the scene of events ought not to be more ignorant of what is going on in our immediate neighbourhood than our friends who are so many thousands of miles removed from it.

I cannot say much of the Coreans, for, in the first place, the usual sources of information are almost silent on the subject, there being about only one reliable English work on Corea; and secondly we have no means, had we the desire, to study this people, who are so jealous of their women that they wont allow you to approach within a mile of their dwellings. On one occasion I remember I sought, for the purposes of this present narrative, to set aside this prohibition, and feigning ignorance of it I penetrated to the outskirts of a village, when half-a-dozen big fellows rushing up to me, and gesticulating, I thought it advisable to "boom off." However, I saw what I had ventured thus far to see, notwithstanding—one of their women; but I am afraid an ugly specimen of the sex. So far does this feeling prevail that they would not permit even our admiral's lady to satisfy a woman's curiosity about women; though the chief of the village did condescend to allow her to sit beside him on his mat, and even went so far as to offer her a *smoke of his pipe*.

One of the accounts of their origin is peculiar. A certain beautiful goddess once descended from the celestial regions and sojourned in Corea. But it would appear that she left her hat behind, for shortly after arrival she received a sun-stroke, which caused her to lay an egg of abnormal size, out of which there stepped—minerva-like—a full blown Corean of gigantic stature. This young fellow, in one of his incursions into the mountains, one day returned to his mamma with a beautiful white-skinned maid whom he had picked up in a fairy bower. His mother was not at all pleased—so the story goes—with this maid of earth, and made it so hot for her that in a fit of rage the son, whom she had hatched with such tender solicitude, slew her. Remorseful at the deed, he swore that henceforth a similar misfortune should never again occur to any man; hence the seclusion of the women. I need scarcely add that from this stalwart first Corean and his pale bride all the present race is descended.

The mandarin at Gen San came on board, attended with great ceremony—flags, banners, pennons, soldiers, and trumpeters, in boat loads; the latter gentlemen being furnished with brass instruments, such as angels are usually depicted with, but which can be made to shut up like a telescope to vary the music. The men are certainly a fine race—tall and upright as an arrow, and rather intelligent looking than otherwise. They wear long coarsely-fabricated, white cotton garments, split up behind, in front and on the hips—all tails in fact; but the great national peculiarity seems to be the hats, some made of bamboo, others of horse hair, of very delicate net-

or gauze work, and shaped like a reversed flower pot with a rim attached. Its purpose cannot be to keep the head warm, to protect it from the rain, or to answer any other purpose to which a hat may be applied: for instance you could not get a drink of water by means of it, nor would it serve as a pillow. The ordinary color of these hats is black, but in consequence of the queen's demise they now don a white one—white being, as in China, the symbol of mourning. Some who cannot afford, or have not the inclination, to purchase a white one, paste a patch of white paper over the crown of the black one which answers the purpose just as well.

They betray a weakness for rum, and a knowledge of the vessels in which it is usually issued on board a man-of-war, scarcely credited of a people who have so few means of acquiring such familiarity. But so it is, and if noses can be accepted as indices of truth in such matters, something stronger than water has been used in tinting them.

The soldiers of the party presented the appearance of guys, rather than men of "fight." What do you say to a mixed uniform of pink and light blue glazed calico, over dingy under-garments of impossible analysis, and a mushroom hat of the coarsest felt, with the distinguishing red horse hair attached to the crown; wooden shot and powder pouches of the roughest and rudest make slung across the shoulders by a piece of thin cord? And such shot! irregular pellets of raw iron and lead, of which all I can say is that dying by such help would be far from an æsthetic operation. And yet these same soldiers, as a mere pastime, are employed in a service which requires no mean bravery. When not fighting the two-legged enemies of their country, they are engaged waging war against the four-legged ones, their land being infested with tigers of great size and strength.

In the evening the local mandarin sent a present of fruits, fowls, eggs, vegetables, and a pig, to the admiral. "Dennis," however, made a terrible fuss at the prospect of being converted into a toothsome dish for the sailors, and sent up such a squeal, in choicest pig-Corean—piercing, prolonged, torturing—that the band was compelled to cease, in the midst of the most pathetic part of "*La Traviata*," out of respect of his superior music.

As the ladies of this country are for ever immured within the four mud walls of their houses, the men have usurped a right generally conceded to females, namely, that of indicating by some sign their state in life— married or single. The married men do their hair up in a knot at the top of the head; those who have not yet seen the girl they like better than themselves wear theirs in a loose trace behind; whilst some others who have successfully passed through both states, and are quite willing to try it again—for marriage amongst them is honorable and universal, as in China—indicate this desire by donning a sort of skull cap. I thought it not a little curious that the men, and not the women, should take the initiative in this matter. Men, in general, after having committed a mistake, don't like to admit it.

After Gen-San we moved a little further south to Chosan, where, scarce had we anchored, when the arrival of a small steamer threw the whole squadron into violent commotion. She had been chartered either by Sir

Thomas Wade or Sir Harry Parkes expressly to convey despatches to the admiral—what the subject was none of us could even guess, though it subsequently leaked out that a disturbance of some sort had broken out at Foo-Choo. The "Zephyr" was at once signalled to raise steam; and all the admiral's staff were warned to hold themselves in readiness to turn over to the "Vigilant" on the following day. Next morning the admiral sailed, preceded by the "Cleopatra" by a few hours, and followed by the "Swift."

September 12th.—We are now at Port Hamilton, and drawing towards the end of our cruise. The "Vigilant" came in this morning with Mrs. Willes on board to witness the regatta got up for the squadron. It was a success in every way—especially so to the crew of our first cutter; in fact a more than average share of prizes fell to "Jumbo." I quote the flag borne by our boats (arms, an elephant passant-argent; motto, "Jumbo"). The sailing races were to have come off the following day, but at daybreak it was blowing so hard, and the barometer falling so rapidly, that a second anchor had to be dropped. On the gale increasing cable was veered; and it went on increasing until a third anchor was let go.

The third day came in fine, with a breeze all that could be desired. To prevent loss of time, and to simplify matters, all the boats, of no matter what race, started at once. It was a pretty sight to witness this mosquito fleet clapping on sail after sail—balloons, outriggers, sky-jibs, and other extraordinary bits of duck. Our second cutter—under the joint control of the commander and Mr. Alexander, midshipman—went around in splendid style, the manœuvring of Mr. Alexander being beyond all praise. She came in first, and carried off the admiral's cup. The whaler was managed equally well by Mr. Patey, and came in an excellent second.

This regatta brought the cruise practically to an end, though each ship has to repair to Chefoo for provisions, independently of the other.

On the passage we ran against something dirty, which succeeded in whipping our main-topsail clean off the yard, and left it dangling by the starboard sheet, at the lower yard-arm; and as misfortunes don't happen singly, the jib made most energetic and partially successful efforts to hang up beside it. It did not reach quite so far aft as that, but it did manage to coil itself around the fore yard arm. Such a terrific squall we have never encountered before. And such lightning and rain! who ever saw the like?

But joyful news was awaiting us at Chefoo. Mr. Robinson, in fulfilment of a promise he made on leaving us at Nagasaki, telegraphed the welcome, long-expected intelligence that the "Audacious" commissioned on the 5th instant.

And now, dear shipmates, I must leave you, and I do so at once regretfully and joyfully; regretfully, that I have to bid farewell to what has given me not a little pleasure to write; joyfully, that I have—as I would fain hope—been enabled to bring my narrative to a successful termination. If any of you are disappointed that I have not pursued it further, think how necessary it was that my manuscript should be in the printer's hands as speedily as possible. I thought no more opportune ending could have offered itself to me than the telegram before quoted.

If "In Eastern Seas" shall have in the slightest degree contributed one pleasure to you or your friends, or shall be the humble instrument of calling to your mind some pleasant memories of the commission, I shall indeed feel amply rewarded for any little trouble I may have been put to in helping you to such pleasure or to such memories.

We have seen many lands together, many and strange peoples, much that is delightful beyond description in this, our beautiful world; but, after all, one feels his soul filled with enthusiasm at the thought that he is an Englishman, though he may be but a sailor. Persons at home scarcely realise what an inheritance that is.

In conclusion, may we all find happy homes; happy mothers, wives, sisters, and sweethearts, all the more willing to treasure us because we have been loyal to them for such a long, long time. I don't drink— as you know —but I don't mind cracking a bottle of lemonade to the future success in life, and happiness of all my late, much-respected, shipmates. God bless them all.

APPENDIX A.

Deaths During the Commission.

NAMES.	RANK OR RATING.	DATE OF DEATH.	PLACE OF DEATH.	CAUSE OF DEATH.
		1878.		
John Bayley	Pte. R.M.	Sept. 13th	Red Sea	Heat Apoplexy
Mr. Easton	Gunner	„ 14th	„	„
Mr. Scoble	Engineer	„ 17th	„	„
E. Dewdney	Boy	Oct. 18th	Singapore	„
		1879.		
Richd. Darcy	Ord.	March 10th	Hong Kong	Fall from Aloft
Hy. Harper	Bandsman	May 10th	Shanghai	Decline
Fredk. Smyth	Stoker	July 3rd	Yokohama	Drowning
Ch. Allen	Ord.	Dec. 11th	Amoy	„
		1880.		
John Irish	A.B.	Oct. 26th	At Sea	„
		1881.		
Wm. Edwards	2d. C.M.T.	April 15th	Hong Kong	General Debility
Wm. Edwards	Boy	June 24th	Chefoo	Fall from Aloft
Wm. McGill	Ord.	Aug. 12th	Vladivostock	„
John Higgins	Pte. R.M.	Novr. 6th	Wosung	Choleraic Diarrhœa
Wm. Young	A.B.	„ 8th	„	„
Wm. Drew *	A.B.	?	Hong Kong	Ruptured Blood-vessel

* Discharged to hospital, and died during our cruise to the north. Date of death not procurable in ship's office.

APPENDIX B.

Table showing places visited and actual distance run, in miles, by H.M.S. "Iron Duke," during commission.

Date of Departure.	From	To	Date of Arrival.	Actual Distance run.
1878.				Miles.
July 25	Plymouth	Portsmouth	July 26	139
August 1	Portsmouth	Plymouth	August 2	150
„ 4	Plymouth	Gibraltar	„ 11	1022
„ 15	Gibraltar	Malta	„ 22	931
„ 25	Malta	Port Said	Septr. 1	865
Septr. 2	Port Said	Suez	„ 4	86
„ 7	Suez	Aden	„ 17	1144
„ 21	Aden	Point de Galle	Octr. 4	1950
Octr. 8	Point de Galle	Singapore	„ 18	1434
Novr. 18	Singapore	Malacca	Novr. 19	100
„ 19	Malacca	Din Ding	„ 21	164
„ 21	Din Ding	Penang	„ 22	102
„ 28	Penang	Din Ding	„ 29	112
„ 30	Din Ding	Singapore	Decr. 2	271
Decr. 5	Singapore	Sarawak	„ 8	368
„ 9	Sarawak	Labuan	„ 12	325
„ 14	Labuan	Manilla	„ 19	724
„ 24	Manilla	Manilla	„ 28	511
„ 31	Manilla	Hong Kong	Jany. 4	640
1879.				
March 11	Hong Kong	Chino Bay	March 12	101
„ 14	Chino Bay	Hong Kong	„ 15	101
April 21	Hong Kong	Merz Bay	April 21	61
„ 22	Merz Bay	Amoy	„ 24	262
„ 26	Amoy	White Dogs	„ 27	152
„ 28	White Dogs	Chusan	„ 30	283
May 5	Chusan	Wosung	May 7	111
„ 23	Wosung	Nagasaki	„ 25	388
June 11	Nagasaki	Takasima	June 12	230
„ 13	Takasima	Sojasima	„ 13	96
„ 14	Sojasima	Kobé	„ 14	39
„ 17	Kobé	Yokohama	„ 19	319
July 24	Yokohama	Yamada	July 25	231
„ 26	Yamada	Awomori	„ 27	200
„ 28	Awomori	Hakodadi	„ 29	53
August 9	Hakodaté	Dui	Augst 15	597
„ 16	Dui	Castries Bay	„ 17	51

Date of Departure.	From	To	Date of Arrival.	Actual Distance run.
Augst. 19	Castries Bay	Barracouta Hr.	Augst. 20	132
,, 23	Barracouta Hr.	Olga Bay	,, 26	380
,, 26	Olga Bay	Askold Is.	,, 27	146
,, 28	Askold Is.	Vladivostock	,, 28	32
,, 31	Vladivostock	Nagasaki	Septr. 4	666
Septr. 7	Nagasaki	Chefoo	,, 12	580
Octr. 18	Chefoo	Takasima	Octr. 23	662
,, 24	Takasima	Sojasima	,, 24	94
,, 25	Sojasima	Kobé	,, 25	48
Novr. 5	Kobé	Yokohama	Novr. 6	346
,, 24	Yokohama	Matson Is.	Decr. 3	1311
Decr. 3	Matson	Amoy	,, 4	185
,, 12	Amoy	Hope Bay	,, 13	132
,, 14	Hope Bay	Hong Kong	,, 15	146
	At Hong Kong	Target Practice		147
1880.				
April 5	Hong Kong	Tong Sha	April 9	423
,, 15	Tong Sha	Chefoo	,, 21	844
May 11	Chefoo	Nagasaki	May 15	581
,, 29	Nagasaki	Yobuko	,, 29	88
,, 31	Yobuko	Himesima	,, 31	109
June 1	Himesima	Obe-hito-ura	June 1	60
,, 2	Obe-hito-ura	Sojasima	,, 2	89
,, 3	Sojasima	Kobé	,, 3	45
,, 9	Kobé	Yokohama	,, 12	364
July 8	Yokohama	Kamaishi	July 10	339
,, 10	Kamaishi	Endermo	,, 12	240
,, 17	Endermo	Hakodadi	,, 17	68
,, 29	Hakodadi	O'Kosiri Island	,, 30	94
August 3	Okisiri Island	Hakodadi	August 3	80
,, 6	Hakodadi	Nagasaki	,, 10	830
,, 11	Nagasaki	Amoy	,, 16	922
,, 17	Amoy	Hong Kong	,, 18	295
Septr. 25	Hong Kong	Amoy	Septr. 27	349
,, 28	Amoy	Nagasaki	Octr. 5	896
Octr. 16	Nagasaki	Sojasima	,, 18	369
,, 19	Sojasima	Kobé	,, 19	51
,, 23	Kobé	Sojasima	,, 23	68
,, 24	Sojasima	Nagasaki	,, 26	312
Decr. 2	Nagasaki	Rugged Isles	Decr. 5	440
,, 10	Rugged Isles	Pirates' Bay	,, 10	10
,, 11	Pirates' Bay	Amoy	,, 14	495
,, 15	Amoy	Hong Kong	,, 17	258

Date of Departure.	From	To	Date of Arrival.	Actual Distance run.
1881.				
Feby. 16	Hong Kong	Singapore	Feby. 24	1415
March 3	Singapore	Malacca	March 4	106
,, 4	Malacca	Din Ding	,, 6	170
,, 6	Din Ding	Penang	,, 7	97
,, 8	Penang	Singapore	,, 11	412
,, 13	Singapore	Cape St. James	,, 17	658
,, 18	Cape St. James	Saigon	,, 18	38
,, 19	Saigon	Hong Kong	,, 25	1067
April 21	Hong Kong	Chino Bay	April 22	148
,, 25	Chino Bay	Tungao Bay	,, 25	33
,, 26	Tungao Bay	Namoa Is.	,, 26	55
,, 30	Namoa Is.	Rees Is.	,, 30	40
May 1	Rees Is.	Amoy	May 1	57
,, 7	Amoy	Lamyet Is.	,, 8	117
,, 13	Lamyet Is.	White Dogs	,, 13	64
,, 14	White Dogs	Matson	,, 14	18
,, 19	Matson	Chefoo	June 6	1269
July 3	Chefoo	Wosung	July 6	467
,, 10	Wosung	Nagasaki	,, 14	426
,, 28	Nagasaki	Tsusima	,, 29	127
,, 31	Tsusima	Posiette Bay	August 7	606
Augst. 11	Posiette Bay	Vladivostock	,, 12.	78
,, 19	Vladivostock	Olga Bay	,, 22	190
,, 29	Olga Bay	St. Vladimir Bay	,, 30	24
Septr. 3	St. Vladimir Bay	Hakodadi	Septr. 7	373
,, 15	Hakodadi *	Yamada	,, 17	239
,, 18	Yamada	Sendai Bay	,, 19	104
,, 20	Sendai Bay	Yokosuka	,, 22	274
,, 24	Yokosuka	Yokohama	,, 24	13
Octr. 2	Yokohama	Kobé	Octr. 4	372
,, 5	Kobé	Sojasima	,, 5	42
,, 6	Sojasima	Gogosima	,, 6	92
,, 7	Gogosima	Himesima	,, 7	51
,, 8	Himesima	Nagasaki	,, 9	210
,, 26	Nagasaki	Wosung	,, 29	448
Novr. 23	Wosung	Hong Kong	Novr. 29	804
1882.				
Feby. 11	Hong Kong	Titam Bay	Feby. 11	22
,, 13	Titam Bay	Titam Bay	,, 13	6
,, 14	Titam Bay	Bogue Forts	,, 14	60
,, 27	Bogue Forts	Hong Kong	,, 27	61

* Touched at Kamaishi *en route.*

Date of Departure.	From	To	Date of Arrival.	Actual Distance run.
1882.				
April 19	Hong Kong	Osima, Loo Choo	May 3	1193
May 11	Osima, Loo Choo	Nagasaki	,, 16	416
,, 27	Nagasaki	Kobé	June 3	532
June 10	Kobé	Kaneda Bay	,, 14	368
,, 15	Kaneda Bay	Yokohama	,, 15	21
July 2	Yokohama	Hakodadi	July 9	665
,, 12	Hakodadi	Castries Bay	,, 22	636
,, 27	Castries Bay	Dui	,, 28	54
,, 30	Dui	Barracouta	,, 31	131
August 4	Barracouta	Vladivostock	Augst 13	480
,, 19	Vladivostock	Gen San *	,, 24	393
,, 30	Gen San	Fusan †	Septr. 3	288
Septr. 7	Fusan	Port Hamilton	,, 8	134
,, 15	Port Hamilton	Chefoo	,, 19	429
Octr. 4	Chefoo	Wosung	Octr. 8	482
,, 20	Wosung	Nagasaki		388
‡	Nagasaki	Hong Kong		1217
Decr. 7	Hong Kong	Singapore		1415
,, 20	Singapore	Point de Galle or Trincomalee		1434
1883.				
‡	Point de Galle	Aden	Jany. 15	1950
Jany. 17	Aden	Suez		1144
‡	Suez	Port Said	,, 27	86
,, 28	Port Said	Malta	Feby. 4	865
Feby. 7	Malta	Gibraltar		931
‡	Gibraltar	Plymouth		1022

Total number of miles made during the commission, 55,566; or a distance equal to 2¼ times around the earth.

* Port Lazaref.   † Cho-San.

‡ The writer assumes that these places will be visited on the voyage home; and—as will be seen by referring to the earlier part of the table—we have touched at the same places before, the same distances are quoted. The dates necessary to make the form complete it is hoped the reader will be able to supply.